Damselflies

Forewings and hindwings similar shape, closed or partially spread at rest. Thin body. Weak fliers.

Broad-winged Damsels	Broad-winged
Spreadwings	Wings clear, partially spread when perched — Spreadwings
Pond Damsels	Wings clear, closed when perched — Pond Damsels

Wings	Red or Orange	Blue	Green	Yellow or Brown	Eye Position	Other Useful Clues	
				BODY MAY HAVE THIS COLOR:			
Clear				Yes		Hillside seeps; rare and local	Petaltails
Clear	Unusual	Yes	Yes	Yes		Large eyes; often multicolored spots on abdomen	Darners
Clear	Unusual		Yes	Yes		Abdomen often clubbed; camouflaged color patterns	Clubtails
Clear				Yes		2–3 yellow side stripes on thorax; green or blue eyes	Spiketails
Clear				Yes		1 yellow side stripe on thorax; very long legs	Cruisers
Clear or with obvious colors or marks			Iridescent	Yes		Mostly brown overall; elusive; often green eyes	Emeralds
Clear or with obvious colors or marks	Yes	Yes	Yes	Yes		Common, conspicuous	Skimmers

Stokes Field Guides

Stokes Field Guide to Birds: Eastern Region

Stokes Field Guide to Birds: Western Region

Stokes Field Guide to Bird Songs: Eastern Region (CD/cassette)

Stokes Field Guide to Bird Songs: Western Region (CD/cassette)

Stokes Beginner's Guides

Stokes Beginner's Guide to Bats

Stokes Beginner's Guide to Birds: Eastern Region

Stokes Beginner's Guide to Birds: Western Region

Stokes Beginner's Guide to Butterflies

Stokes Beginner's Guide to Dragonflies

Stokes Beginner's Guide to Shorebirds

Stokes Backyard Nature Books

Stokes Bird Feeder Book

Stokes Bird Gardening Book

Stokes Birdhouse Book

Stokes Bluebird Book

Stokes Butterfly Book

Stokes Hummingbird Book

Stokes Oriole Book

Stokes Purple Martin Book

Stokes Wildflower Book: East of the Rockies

Stokes Wildflower Book: From the Rockies West

Stokes Nature Guides

Stokes Guide to Amphibians and Reptiles

Stokes Guide to Animal Tracking and Behavior

Stokes Guide to Bird Behavior, Volume 1

Stokes Guide to Bird Behavior, Volume 2

Stokes Guide to Bird Behavior, Volume 3

Stokes Guide to Enjoying Wildflowers

Stokes Guide to Nature in Winter

Stokes Guide to Observing Insect Lives

Other Stokes Books

The Natural History of Wild Shrubs and Vines

STOKES
Beginner's Guide
to Dragonflies and Damselflies

Blair Nikula, Jackie Sones   *with Donald and Lillian Stokes*

Little, Brown and Company
Boston   New York   London

First Edition

For information on Time Warner Trade
Publishing's online publishing program,
visit www.ipublish.com.

10 9 8 7 6 5 4 3 2 1

TWP

Library of Congress Cataloging-in-Publication Data
Nikula, Blair
    Stokes beginner's guide to dragonflies and
damselflies / by Blair Nikula and Jackie Sones
with Donald and Lillian Stokes. — 1st. ed.
        p.   cm.
    ISBN 0-316-81679-5
    1. Dragonflies — Identification. 2. Damsel-
flies — Identification. I. Title: Beginner's
guide to dragonflies and damselflies. II. Sones,
Jackie. III. Stokes, Donald W. IV. Title.

QL520.N55 2001
595.7'33 — dc21   2001029239

Printed in Singapore

Contents

Foreword

Dragonflies and damselflies are immensely popular, and recently there has been a huge surge of interest in these magical winged insects. Their striking silhouettes decorate countless gift items from jewelry to birdbaths, from fabrics to garden ornaments. Rarely has something in nature been so widely depicted while at the same time remained so little known to the public.

From nature lovers to birdwatchers, from kids to adults, dragonflies and damselflies enthrall us all. You cannot help being drawn to their gossamer jeweled wings, their brilliant colors, their exciting behavior, and most of all their spectacular aerial abilities. But when it comes to dragonflies and damselflies, we are almost all beginners, for until now there has not existed an introductory guide to help us learn about them on a national basis.

So this *Stokes Beginner's Guide to Dragonflies and Damselflies* is a first, a truly creative, well-organized, authoritative, and user-friendly guide to some of nature's most intriguing creatures. We asked Blair Nikula and Jackie Sones, two superb naturalists and dragonfly experts, to write this beginner's guide to more than 100 of the most common species to be found across North America.

The innovative identification table in the front of the book will quickly enable you to identify and learn about the species you see in your backyard and farther afield. And the stunning photographs and clearly organized text will help lead you to an appreciation of the behavior and lives of these amazing animals.

We hope this guide opens up a whole new world for you, the fascinating world of dragonflies and damselflies. Ebony Jewelwings, Aurora Damsels, Variable Dancers, Stream Cruisers, Elfin Skimmers, and Sedge Sprites — these are just some of the dragonflies and damselflies that await you. Go outside and start to discover and enjoy them.

Yours in nature,
Don and Lillian Stokes

Introduction

Through art and folklore, dragonflies and damselflies have been a part of human culture since at least 300 B.C. Although people have been fascinated with dragonflies and damselflies for thousands of years, there are few field guides available to help beginners identify them. This book provides clear written descriptions, full-color photographs, and a step-by-step process for field identification.

Dragonflies and damselflies are spectacular creatures. We are drawn to their beautiful colors and intriguing body designs. Their speed and fascinating behaviors attract our attention. Their relatively large size and presence in almost every wetland make them very easy to observe. During a short visit to a pond on a warm summer day, it is possible to see dragonflies zipping by at 20 miles an hour, darting aggressively after rival males, capturing and devouring other insects while on the wing, searching for mates, laying eggs, and outmaneuvering the jaws of lunging fish!

In this book we describe more than 100 of the approximately 435 species of dragonflies and damselflies found in North America. Most of the species included are common, widespread, and conspicuous. However, we also show at least one representative of each family and major genus. Our goal is not only to help you identify the dragonflies and damselflies that you are most likely to see, but also to introduce you to the diversity of these amazing insects. By doing so we hope we encourage you to spend more time outdoors, enjoying and protecting nearby ponds and lakes, rivers and streams, bogs, swamps, and marshes — the habitats dragonflies and damselflies call home.

Life Cycle and Behavior

Dragonflies and damselflies are members of the insect order Odonata, a group that has inhabited the earth for more than 250 million years. Presently there are approximately 5,000 species recognized worldwide. They are large insects with three major body parts: head, thorax, and abdomen. The head has two large compound eyes, three simple eyes, two inconspicuous antennae, and toothed jaws. The thorax supports six legs and four membranous wings. The segmented abdomen is long and slender. (Their basic anatomy is illustrated inside the back cover of this book.)

Dragonflies and damselflies have a three-part life cycle, including **egg,**

Pair of Yellow-legged Meadowhawks in copulation wheel (female below)

larva (also called nymph or naiad), and **adult.**

Once mature, adult dragonflies and damselflies are very active near water. Their aerial abilities — impressive speed and agility (flying forward and backward, gliding, and hovering) — are unsurpassed. Males of some species establish fixed **territories** for mating or

feeding, which may range in size from less than 1 square yard up to 100 or cover a 2–50-yard stretch along a river. Territory size varies between species and among individuals and also may be dependent upon the density of males and the quality of the habitat. Watch for patrolling males defending their territories by actively chasing other males and females.

Mating and Egg Laying

You may observe **tandem pairs,** when the male uses his abdominal appendages to clasp the female behind the eyes (dragonflies) or by the neck (damselflies). This tandem position is a precursor to mating and also may be maintained after mating and during egg laying. **Mating pairs** form a "copulation wheel," a position unique to dragonflies and damselflies. In this position,

Tandem pair of Sweetflag Spreadwing damselflies, female (below) depositing eggs in plant stem

the male transfers a packet of sperm to the female (a process that takes from 3 seconds to over an hour). A male dragonfly also has the unusual ability to remove sperm deposited by a previous male to insure that his own sperm are the ones fertilizing the female's eggs!

Soon after mating, females lay their eggs (**oviposit**) in the water, in bottom sediments, or in aquatic plants (stems or leaves that are emergent, floating, or submerged). Females have the ability to store sperm for long periods of time (perhaps their lifetimes), and the eggs are fertilized just before they are laid. During egg laying, the male may remain in tandem with the female (called contact guarding), he may release the female and hover nearby (noncontact guarding), or he may abandon the female. Each female may deposit hundreds or thousands of eggs during several different episodes of egg laying. Eggs vary in size, shape, and color. Most are very small (less than 1 millimeter — about 0.04 inch — in length) and spherical or cylindrical. They can be white, yellow, orange, brown, green, or gray. The egg stage typically lasts from 1 to 8 weeks (varies with the species and temperature), although some eggs overwinter, that is, their development is delayed during the winter and completed in the spring.

Larval Development

Larvae emerge from the eggs and spend their lives growing and developing underwater. Dragonfly larvae obtain oxygen through 60 to 80 gills located inside the abdomen, while damselflies use three long tail-like projections (caudal lamellae) at the end of the abdomen.

In the insect world, full-grown dragonfly and damselfly larvae are relatively large, ranging from 0.25 to over 2 inches in length. The larval stage

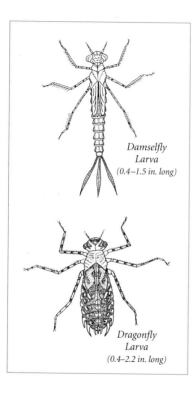

Damselfly Larva
(0.4–1.5 in. long)

Dragonfly Larva
(0.4–2.2 in. long)

A newly emerged adult dragonfly (teneral) with exuvia (its last larval skeleton)

persists for 1 month to 5 years (!) depending upon the species and environmental conditions.

Larvae are either sit-and-wait preda-tors or active hunters and detect their prey by sight, touch, or vibration. They use their specialized extendable lower lips (equipped with hooks) to capture aquatic insects (especially fly larvae) as well as crustaceans, worms, snails, tadpoles, and small fish. Fish, birds, frogs, turtles, and other insects in turn eat the larvae.

They grow via **molting** and shed their exoskeletons, or shells, 8 to 17 times before becoming adults. When the time is right, dragonfly and damselfly larvae undergo an incredible **metamorphosis,** leaving their underwater worlds to become winged masters of the air. The larva crawls to a terrestrial support (for example, a plant stem, tree trunk, rock, or riverbank) and emerges from the last larval skeleton as an adult. Cast skeletons, called **exuviae,** are often found clinging to wetland vegetation.

Feeding, Migration, and Other Behaviors

The newly emerged adult is called a **teneral;** its wings and body are soft, shiny, and pale yellowish green in color. It takes a few days to a few weeks for the body and wings to harden and develop their true colors. During this time dragonflies and damselflies depend on upland habitats, such as grasslands and woodlands, for shelter and food.

As with the larvae, adult dragonflies and damselflies are opportunistic **predators;** they'll eat just about anything they can catch! They prey upon a variety of insects (flies, midges, ants, butterflies, moths, other dragonflies and damselflies), and one species has even been known to capture hummingbirds. Dragonflies usually chase flying insects, while damselflies often glean perched insects directly from vegetation.

Golden-winged Skimmer eating a spreadwing damselfly.

In general, adults live only 2 to 4 weeks. They fall prey to birds (flycatchers, swallows, falcons, kites), frogs, fish, spiders, other insects, and even carnivorous plants such as sundews.

Exceptions in adult longevity include some tropical species and migrant dragonflies, which may live for months. In North America, approximately 16 species in two families (darners and skimmers) are known to be migratory. These species have been observed in situations very similar to bird and butterfly migrations (large numbers of individuals exhibiting strong, persistent unidirectional movements, often associated with favorable weather conditions).

The stimuli causing these migratory movements have not yet been determined, but may include parasites and environmental conditions (drought, for example). As in Monarch butterflies, the individual dragonflies that fly south in the fall will not return in the spring. Northbound migrants are at least one generation removed from southbound migrants. At present, the exact origins and destinations of these migrant dragonflies are unclear, as are the total distances covered and the time it takes to fly those distances. Dragonfly migration is a wide-open field of discovery!

Along with migration, other interesting dragonfly and damselfly behaviors to look for in the field are related to regulating body temperature (thermoregulation). Because they require a minimum temperature to fly, adult dragonflies and damselflies depend on external (and in some species, internal) sources of heat. You may see them **basking** (perched at an angle that maximizes surface area exposed to the sun) or **wing whirring** (rapid beating of wings, similar to shivering, which generates heat). At other times, when the adults need to cool off, you may see them **obelisking** (holding their abdomens almost straight up in the air in order to reduce exposure to the sun), perching in the shade, or dunking in the water.

Little Blue Dragonlet in obelisking position

Identifying Dragonflies and Damselflies

The easiest way to approach the identification of dragonflies and damselflies is to do a little studying first. Read through the observation tips on pages 18–19. Learn the basic anatomy described on the inside back cover. Look over the Quick Guide to Families on pages 30–39. Knowing the basics will help you move forward more quickly.

A Step-by-Step Approach

- **Begin your adventure.** Find a dragonfly or damselfly (try a nearby pond). Watch it carefully. Answer the questions listed under What to Look For (see page 14). It may be helpful to record your observations and to draw a sketch in a notebook.

- **Determine whether it is a damselfly or a dragonfly.** Use the Identification Table on the inside front cover and the comparative descriptions on page 15.

- **Place it in a family.** The Identification Table on the inside front cover and the Quick Guide to Families will help you determine which family your insect belongs to. Use the color tabs to locate the species descriptions for that family.

- **Locate the group that it looks most like within the family.** Similar-looking species are grouped together within each color tab section. Simply flip through the pages to narrow down your choices.

- **Find a match.** Compare the photographs, read through the descriptions, and check the range maps to decide between species with similar color patterns.

If you can't find an exact match, you might have a species not included in this book. In that case, some of the regional guides listed in the Resources section on page 25 might be helpful. You will not be able to identify every individual you see. Although many dragonflies and damselflies are readily identifiable in the field, there are many others that can only be identified in the hand or under a microscope. Don't let this frustrate you — even the experts let many pass unidentified!

What to Look For

It's helpful to think about the identification of dragonflies and damselflies as a process that starts with knowing what to look for. Listed below are some basic questions to ask yourself every time you look at a dragonfly or damselfly. (Some of the terms may seem strange to you now, but they will become familiar with practice.)

Behavior — Is it perched? If so, how and where? Horizontally on a rock? Hanging vertically from a branch? Does it fly high or low, among vegetation or in the open? Does it spend more of its time perched or flying? How is it interacting with other dragonflies?

Wings — When it is perched, are the wings held closed over the back or out to the sides? Are there any markings on the wings? If so, where are they? What shape and size and color? Note that almost all dragonflies and damselflies have small rectangular markings, called stigmas (or pterostigmas), near the tip of each wing. Occasionally the size, shape, and color of the stigmas are helpful for identification.

Abdomen — What is the primary color on the abdomen? What are the other colors? Are there stripes or spots or rings? What segments do they occur on? Methodically check segments 1–10 for their color patterns (the numbering of segments is shown on the inside back cover of this book). If possible, look at the shapes of the abdominal appendages (see page 21).

Thorax — What is the primary color on the thorax? Are there stripes or spots? If so, are they on the top (dorsal surface), the shoulders, or the sides (lateral surface)? How many are there? What color, shape, and size are they?

Eyes and Face — Are the eyes small or large? When viewed from above, are they separate or do they meet in the middle of the head? Do they meet broadly along a seam or at one point? What color are they? If it is a damselfly, are there eyespots (colored spots on top of the head behind the eyes)? What size, shape, and color are they? What color is the face?

Legs — Are the legs short or long? What color are they? Do they have noticeable spines?

Damselflies vs. Dragonflies

One of the first steps in identifying odonates in the field is to decide whether an individual is a damselfly or a dragonfly. Look for these key features to tell them apart:

- **Wing shape:** In damselflies, the forewings and hindwings are similar in shape. In dragonflies, the hindwings are broader than the forewings.
- **Wing position:** When perched, damselflies hold their wings pressed together over their backs or partially spread, while dragonflies hold their wings straight out to the sides.
- **Overall appearance:** Damselflies tend to be smaller and more slender than dragonflies.

- **Eye position:** The compound eyes of damselflies are separated by a distance greater than the eye diameter, while those of most dragonflies meet in the middle of the head. (Note the exceptions of petaltails and clubtails. Their eyes are separate, but the distance between them is less than the eye diameter.)
- **Flight style:** Damselflies are weak fliers, staying low to the ground, near the water's surface, or among vegetation. Dragonflies are stronger, faster, and typically are found flying out in the open.

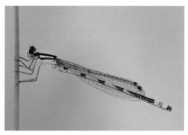

Damselfly (Marsh Bluet)

Dragonfly (Widow Skimmer)

A Closer Look at the Identification Table

The Identification Table and Color Tab Index at the very front of the book are designed to help you make an identification quickly. First, decide whether the insect in question is a damselfly or dragonfly by comparing its appearance to the two main illustrations.

If it is a damselfly, look at wing coloration and wing position when perched to decide which of the three listed families it belongs to. Then follow the appropriate color tab to the species descriptions for that family.

If it is a dragonfly, look at as many of the characteristics listed in the table as possible: overall size, flight pattern, wing coloration, and so on. Compare what you see with the table and use a process of elimination to decide which of the seven listed families it belongs to. Turn to the corresponding color tab pages and flip through them to identify your specimen.

If you only get a quick view and aren't able to see enough characteristics to narrow down the possibilities to one family, scan through the photographs to see if you can find a species with a similar color pattern.

Here are some explanations of the characteristics in the dragonfly table.

Size — Size refers to overall length, from the face to the tip of the abdomen, including the abdominal appendages. In the table, S = Small (1–1.5 inches), M = Medium (1.5–2.5 inches), and L = Large (2.5–4 inches).

Perchers or Fliers — Dragonflies tend to exhibit characteristic flight patterns. Perchers spend a lot of time perched, making only brief flights before landing again (which makes them easy to observe!). Fliers, on the other hand, spend a lot of time flying continuously and are thus more difficult to observe.

Flight Height —Flight height refers to the distance above the ground or water's surface: Low = 0–3 feet, Medium = 3–6 feet, High = over 6 feet.

Perched Position — Dragonflies adopt one of five characteristic postures when they perch. In many cases these postures serve as useful identification clues.

Vertical, on a flat surface

 Vertical, hanging from above

 Oblique

 Horizontal, on a flat surface

 Horizontal, at the tip ("teed up")

tails) in which the eyes do not meet broadly along a seam.

 Meeting broadly along a seam

 Meeting at one point

 Widely separate

Eye Position — Compared to their body size, the compound eyes of dragonflies are enormous. The eyes make up a good portion of the head. Dragonflies are very visual creatures, and their large eyes allow them to see in almost every direction. When viewed from above, there are three basic eye positions. There are three dragonfly families (petaltails, clubtails, and spike-

Other Useful Clues — Here we note miscellaneous features (habitat, status, physical characteristics) that can aid in identification.

Observation Tips

Practice, practice, practice. The more time you spend in the field, the better developed your identification skills will be. Because insects are small and often similar in appearance, it takes a long time to learn about them. Here are some hints to help you get the most from your field experiences.

- **Study anatomy and learn family characteristics.** Know what features to look for and where to look for them.
- **Pay attention to the weather.** Your field trips will be most productive on warm sunny days with little wind.
- **Pack the essentials.** Be sure to take along sunscreen, drinking water, and snacks. Wear shoes (or rubber boots) and pants that you don't mind getting wet.
- **Explore a variety of wetlands.** To see a diversity of species, visit a variety of wetlands. Remember that habitat type can be an important clue for identification. Because ponds support a nice variety of conspicuous species, they are often good places for beginners to start.
- **Go out in different seasons and at different times of day.** A few species are active year-round (especially in the South), but most have short flight periods that are specific to a particular season (spring, early to mid-summer, late summer to early fall). Although activity is greatest from midmorning to midafternoon, some species are crepuscular (more active at dawn or dusk).
- **Observe carefully and record your observations.** Look for as many field marks as possible. Watch for interesting behaviors. Keep a field journal with notes and sketches. Recording what you see forces you to look harder and makes it easier to remember details.
- **Participate in field trips.** Learning from others is one of the fastest ways to make progress. Check program listings at your local nature centers. Read the Dragonfly Society of the Americas newsletter, *Argia*. Some states have Atlas Proj-

ects in which you can participate and contribute to what is known about dragonflies and damselflies in your state.

- **Invest in useful equipment.** Binoculars, particularly those that focus closely (5–6 feet); an aerial insect net (we recommend a net with a 3-foot handle and 15-inch rim); and a magnifying lens (10X) are particularly helpful.

Catching and Releasing Dragonflies and Damselflies

We believe everyone's goal should be, whenever possible, to develop the skills necessary to identify dragonflies and damselflies without catching them. However, when you are first learning about dragonflies it is very helpful to see some of the field marks up close. Also, there are some difficult species for which in-the-hand examination will always be necessary for accurate identification.

To catch them, swing up with your insect net from behind and slightly below. Follow through to force the dragonfly into the narrow end of the net. Flip your wrist to create a fold in the net over the rim; this will prevent the dragonfly from escaping. Reach in and find the wings. (Contrary to popular belief, dragonflies cannot sting!) Using your first two fingers, gently raise all four wings and press them together over the thorax. Carefully disentangle legs or mouthparts from the net. Examine briefly with a hand lens. When you are finished, release the dragonfly into the air or onto a perch. Dragonflies can also be viewed in transparent jars or plastic bags. Be careful of exposure to the sun's heat and damage to their wings.

Note: Because of the lack of information regarding the effects of insect repellent and sunscreen on dragonflies and damselflies, it is best to wash your hands before handling them.

In general, you are likely to encounter more males than females. At wetlands, males are actively defending territories and searching for females. Females, on the other hand, are much less conspicuous and visit wetlands only briefly when they are ready to mate and lay eggs.

Use the following characteristics to help determine whether the individual is a male or female.

- **Color pattern:** In some species, males and females are different colors. In general, males are more colorful than females. Immature males often look like mature females.
- **Abdomen shape:** Females tend to have thicker, more cylindrical abdomens. When viewed from above, the width of the female's abdomen remains fairly constant from the base (nearest the thorax) to the tip, while a male's abdomen often tapers from the base to the tip or is constricted at the base.
- **Behavior:** Some males are territorial and very active at breeding sites. When a pair is flying in tandem, the male is in front and the female is in back. When a pair is in the wheel position, the male is above and the female is below. Only the females will be ovipositing (egg laying).
- **Abdominal appendages:** Males have well-developed, species-specific appendages at the tip of the abdomen. Male dragonflies have 3 appendages (2 superior and 1 inferior), while male damselflies have 4 (2 superior and 2 inferior). Female dragonflies and damselflies have 2 abdominal appendages (often shorter than the male's) and an ovipositor or a subgenital plate underneath the last few segments of the abdomen. Male dragonflies and damselflies also have accessory genitalia at the base of the abdomen, which are visible as a small bump or protrusion underneath segment 2. Abdominal appendages may be visible only through close-focusing binoculars or in the hand.

Male and Female Abdominal Appendages

**Male Dragonfly
(top and side views)**

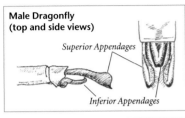

Superior Appendages

Inferior Appendages

**Male Damselfly
(top and side views)**

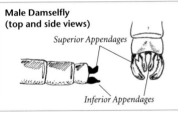

Superior Appendages

Inferior Appendages

Female Dragonfly (side views)

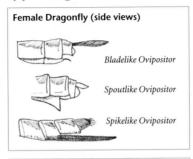

Bladelike Ovipositor

Spoutlike Ovipositor

Spikelike Ovipositor

Female Damselfly (side view)

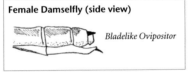

Bladelike Ovipositor

Species Arrangement — To the extent possible, we have grouped similar-looking species together, while maintaining taxonomic integrity. Thus, species are grouped first by family (in the order listed in the Identification Table on the inside cover), then by genus, then by coloration of the males.

Common Names — Common and scientific names used in this book are those established by the Dragonfly Society of the Americas and published in *A Checklist of North American Odonata* (Slater Museum of Natural History, 1999).

Measurements — The number beneath the name refers to overall length (including abdominal appendages). This represents an average; individuals can vary slightly.

Photographs — Whenever possible, photographs were chosen based on how well they illustrated key identification features. Females are shown only when they are appreciably different from the males or from other illustrated females.

Identification — The I.D. sections describe the obvious field marks of each species. The most important features are boldfaced. Some characteristics are apparent only at very close range through close-focusing binoculars or in the hand. When we say a species is not identifiable in the field, we mean in-the-hand examination is necessary.

Descriptions begin with the thorax, then proceed to the abdomen, wings, eyes, face, and legs. If a body part has no obvious or significant markings or coloration (for example, clear unmarked wings), that part is excluded from the description.

Markings on the thorax include dorsal (top) stripes and spots, shoulder stripes, and lateral (side) stripes and spots. The abdomen may have stripes, spots, or rings. In some cases, the color of the abdominal appendages is significant. Wing markings, aside from the stigmas, include spots, patches, bars, and bands, and can be of various colors. **Spots** are generally small and more or less rounded. **Patches** are larger and irregularly shaped. **Bars** are narrow and run lengthwise on the wing. **Bands** extend across the wing, from front to back. In some cases, the color and shape of the stigmas can be useful.

Many of the pond damsels have eyespots (colored spots on the top of the head behind the eyes), the size, shape, and color of which can be helpful for identification. Refer to the illustrations on this page and on the inside of the back cover to learn the terminology.

For some of the more difficult groups (the common spreadwings, bluets, and meadowhawks, for instance), we describe key features and discuss identification problems in separate text boxes.

Behavior — This section emphasizes behaviors that assist in identification, such as flight characteristics and manner of perching. Each species is characterized as either a percher or a flier. Perchers tend to make brief flights at low (under 6 feet) heights. Fliers spend long periods on the wing, often at considerable height.

Habitat — A brief habitat description tells you in general terms where each species is found. Much remains to be learned about the specific habitat requirements of most dragonflies and damselflies.

Flight Season — This section provides a very general description of when the adult stage of each species is on the wing. For species that occur across a wide latitudinal range, the flight season can vary tremendously. A species that flies for only a month or so in northern climes may fly for several months in the South, or even year-round in southern Florida. Thus, seasonal terms in this section should be interpreted loosely, taking into account the climate in the reader's region of interest.

Maps — Although much has been learned recently about the distribution

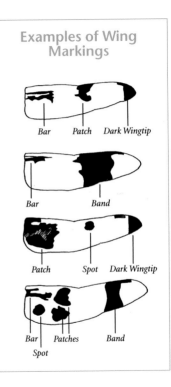

Examples of Wing Markings

Bar   Patch   Dark Wingtip

Bar   Band

Patch   Spot   Dark Wingtip

Bar | Patches   Band
Spot

of dragonflies and damselflies, the exact ranges for most species are still rather poorly known. The small maps accompanying the species accounts are intended to give only a very general sense of each species' distribution.

For the conterminous United States and the Canadian provinces of Newfoundland, Nova Scotia, and New Brunswick, if a species has been recorded from a state or province, that entire state or province is colored on the map. In Alaska and the northern reaches of Canada, where this would result in a grossly distorted depiction of the northern extent of many ranges, only those portions where a species is known to occur are colored in. In these instances we relied upon data generously supplied by Nick Donnelly from his North American county mapping project, which is still in progress.

For a few highly migratory species in which individuals occasionally wander far from their normal ranges, states and provinces where they occur primarily as vagrants are marked with hatching. Admittedly, our simplified methods for constructing these maps result in portraits of species' ranges that are coarse and very liberal. The maps should be interpreted as showing not only where a species is known to occur, but also where it might reasonably occur.

Field Guides

Checklist of Kansas Dragonflies and **Checklist of Kansas Damselflies.** Roy Beckemeyer and Donald Huggins. Emporia, Kans.: Emporia State University, 1997 and 1998.

A Color Guide to Common Dragonflies of Wisconsin. Karl and Dorothy Legler and Dave Westover. Sauk City, Wis.: Karl Legler, 1998.

Common Dragonflies of California: A Beginner's Pocket Guide. Kathy Biggs. Sebastopol, Calif.: Azalea Creek Publishing, 2000.

Damselflies of Florida, Bermuda, and the Bahamas. Sidney Dunkle. Gainesville, Fla.: Scientific Publishers, 1990.

The Dragonflies and Damselflies of Algonquin Provincial Park. Matt Holder. Whitney, Ontario: The Friends of Algonquin Park, 1996.

Dragonflies and Damselflies of Cape Cod. Virginia Carpenter. Brewster, Mass.: Cape Cod Museum of Natural History, 1991.

Dragonflies of the Florida Peninsula, Bermuda, and the Bahamas. Sidney Dunkle. Gainesville, Fla.: Scientific Publishers, 1989.

Dragonflies of Washington. Dennis Paulson. Seattle: Seattle Audubon Society, 1999.

Dragonflies Through Binoculars. Sidney Dunkle. New York: Oxford University Press, 2000.

Manuals

Damselflies of North America. Minter Westfall and Michael May. Gainesville, Fla.: Scientific Publishers, 1996.

Dragonflies: Behavior and Ecology of Odonata. Philip Corbet. Ithaca, N.Y.: Cornell University Press, 1999.

Dragonflies of North America. James Needham, Minter Westfall, and Michael May. Gainesville, Fla.: Scientific Publishers, 2000.

Video

Common Dragonflies of the Northeast. Richard Walton and Richard Forster. Concord, Mass.: Brownbag Productions, 1997.

The Internet

Odonata Information Network
(http://www.afn.org/~iori)
Odonata Listserve. Join by
e-mailing Dennis Paulson at
dpaulson@ups.edu.

Organization

Dragonfly Society of the Americas
This organization publishes a
quarterly newsletter, *Argia,* with
announcements about meetings and
field trips throughout North
America. For more information
contact Nick Donnelly at 2091
Partridge Lane, Binghamton, NY
13903.

Acknowledgments

We dedicate this book to Dick Forster, an incredible friend and field naturalist, without whose enthusiasm and intense commitment to natural history the book might not have happened. We've never laughed or learned so much as we did with him.

Dennis Paulson reviewed the text and made many invaluable improvements. Roy Beckemeyer, Bob Behrstock, and Sarah Jennings also provided helpful suggestions.

We would never have come so far in our learning about dragonflies without inspiration from Ginger Brown. We are also indebted to Bob Barber, Nick Donnelly, Sid Dunkle, and Chris Leahy for so generously sharing their considerable knowledge through the years.

Special thanks to Jeremiah Trimble for his enthusiasm, persistence, companionship, and amazing net! Our dragonfly adventures have taken us to many locations and introduced us to many people. To Dick Walton, Stu Tingley, Michael Veit, Rick Heil, and our many other friends and field companions, thanks for all of the good times, and here's looking forward to many more! We would also like to thank our families, friends, and coworkers for their support and encouragement. And to acknowledge the gift we have all been given to enjoy the natural world around us.

Finally, thanks to Don and Lillian Stokes for their patience and guidance throughout this project, and for recognizing that it was time for a beginner's guide!

Photo Credits

All illustrations by Jacqueline Sones.
All photographs except the following
are by Blair Nikula (T=top, B=bottom,
L=left, R=right):

John Abbott: 100, 135B
Jim Bangma: 44T, 121
Roy Beckemeyer: 116
Robert Behrstock: 66, 73, 98, 122T,
    125T, 133L, 138, 139B, 143B
Dave Czaplak: 72
Sidney Dunkle: 34, 39, 45, 62, 68B, 80,
    82, 88R, 89, 91, 106, 108, 122B, 124,
    139T, 150

Carl Freeman: 151
Ellis Laudermilk: 64T, 69
Dennis Paulson: 47
Jane Ruffin: 81, 120B, 143T
Netta Smith: 127B
Jacqueline Sones: 37, 104, 127T
Michael Veit: 38, 109

A Quick Guide
to Families

Broad-winged Damsel Family
Calopterygidae

Size: Medium

Wings: Broad wings, with complete or partial coloration; butterfly-like flight pattern

Coloration: Often with stunning iridescent coloration (green, blue, or red) on thorax and abdomen

Eyes: Black or brown

Perch: Horizontally, often on streamside vegetation or rocks

Flight: Perchers; fly at low to medium heights

Habitat: Associated with streams and rivers

Miscellaneous: Long spindly legs; females lay eggs in plants with the male guarding nearby; males perform courtship displays

Ebony Jewelwing, Male

8 species (2 genera) in North America
4 species (2 genera) in this guide (see pp. 42–45)

Common Names of Genera in This Guide: Jewelwings, rubyspots

Spreadwing Family
Lestidae

Size: Small to medium

Wings: Most with clear wings; some with an amber wash; held partially spread when perched

Coloration: Often with metallic coloration (green or bronze) on abdomen; often pruinosity (waxlike coating, often whitish in color) on thorax or tip of abdomen; often with blue face

Eyes: Often blue in males and brown in females

Perch: Obliquely

Flight: Perchers; fly at low heights

Habitat: Ponds, marshes, temporary pools, streams; often associated with dense emergent vegetation

Miscellaneous: Long slender abdomens; females lay eggs in plants while in tandem with the male or while alone

Common Spreadwing, Male

18 species (2 genera) in North America
6 species (2 genera) in this guide (see pp. 46–52)

Common Names of Genera in This Guide: Common spreadwings (*Lestes* spp.), great spreadwings (*Archilestes* spp.)

Pond Damsel Family
Coenagrionidae

Size: Small to medium

Wings: Most with clear wings; short stigmas

Coloration: Often brightly colored with blue, green, red, orange, yellow, purple; females of some species with several color forms

Eyes: Often colorful; shape and size of eyespots useful for identification

Perch: Horizontally or obliquely, on vegetation, rocks, or the ground

Flight: Perchers; fly at low heights

Habitat: Common in a variety of habitats: ponds, lakes, bogs, and streams

Miscellaneous: Most common, diverse, and easily observed damselfly group; short legs; females lay eggs in plants while alone, in tandem with the male, or with the male guarding

Azure Bluet, Male

nearby; male abdominal appendages important for identification

96 species (13 genera) in North America
26 species (8 genera) in this guide (see pp. 53–78)

Common Names of Genera in This Guide: Aurora Damsel, bluets, dancers, firetails, forktails, red damsels, sprites

Petaltail Family
Petaluridae

Gray Petaltail, Male

Size: Large

Wings: Clear, with long narrow stigmas

Coloration: Gray and black or yellow and black

Eyes: Widely separated; brown or gray

Perch: Vertically on tree trunks; occasionally horizontally on ground or rocks

Flight: Perchers; fly at low to medium heights

Habitat: Associated with seeps

Miscellaneous: Rare and local; females have bladelike ovipositors and lay eggs in leaves; nymph is semiterrestrial, living in mucky seeps

2 species (2 genera) in North America
1 species (1 genus) in this guide (see p. 79)

Common Name of Genus in This Guide: Gray Petaltail

Darner Family
Aeshnidae

Size: Medium to large

Wings: Most with clear wings; some with amber wash or small brown patch at base of hindwings; wings long

Coloration: Multicolored (brown, with blues, greens, and yellows; occasionally red or purple)

Eyes: Large, meet broadly along a seam; often blue, green, or brown

Perch: Most hang vertically or obliquely from branches; occasionally perch on tree trunks

Flight: Fliers; fly at low to high heights

Habitat: Wide variety of habitats: ponds, lakes, marshes, bogs, sluggish streams; may feed in swarms over fields and clearings

Miscellaneous: Long abdomen; swift fliers; females have bladelike ovipositors and usually lay eggs in plants while alone; some species are migratory

Common Green Darner, Male

39 species (11 genera) in North America
10 species (6 genera) in this guide (see pp. 80–91)

Common Names of Genera in This Guide: Cyrano Darner, green darners (*Anax* spp.), mosaic darners (*Aeshna* spp.), spotted darners (*Boyeria* spp.), Springtime Darner, Swamp Darner

Clubtail Family
Gomphidae

Cobra Clubtail, Male

Size: Small to large

Wings: Most with clear wings; some with amber wash or small brown patch at base of hindwings

Coloration: Camouflaged color patterns (brown or black with yellow, green, or gray)

Eyes: Widely separated; often green or blue

Perch: Horizontally on the ground, rocks, logs, leaves

Flight: Perchers (but males of some species make long patrolling flights); fly at low to medium heights

Habitat: Rivers and streams, some lakes and ponds

Miscellaneous: Flare ("club") at the end of the abdomen (most pronounced in males); abdominal appendages important for identification; some rare and elusive, with short flight periods (often early in the season); females lack ovipositors and lay eggs in water while alone

97 species (13 genera) in North America
9 species (7 genera) in this guide (see pp. 92–101)

Common Names of Genera in This Guide: Common clubtails (*Gomphus* spp.), Dragonhunter, pond clubtails (*Arigomphus* spp.), ringtails, sanddragons, snaketails, spinylegs

Spiketail Family
Cordulegastridae

Size: Large

Wings: Clear

Coloration: Striking black or brown and yellow; two (or three) lateral thoracic stripes

Eyes: Meet at one point; usually green or blue

Perch: Hang obliquely or vertically from branches

Flight: Fliers; fly at low to medium heights

Habitat: Streams, small rivers, brooks, seepages

Miscellaneous: Long slender abdomens; often occur in low densities; males typically fly lengthy patrols up and down streams; females have spikelike ovipositors and lay eggs in bottom sediments while alone

8 species (1 genus) in North America
1 species (1 genus) in this guide (see pp. 102–103)

Common Name of Genus in This Guide: Spiketail

Twin-spotted Spiketail, Female

36

Cruiser Family
Macromiidae

Size: Medium to large

Wings: Most with clear wings; some with small brown patch at base of hindwings

Coloration: Brown or black, with yellow spots on abdomen; one lateral thoracic stripe; face striped with yellow

Eyes: Meet broadly along a seam; those of most river cruisers are bright green

Perch: Hang vertically or obliquely from branches

Flight: Fliers; fly at low to high heights

Habitat: Rivers and large lakes; may also be seen over roads or clearings

Miscellaneous: Very long legs; swift fliers; females lack ovipositors and lay eggs in water while alone

9 species (2 genera) in North America
2 species (2 genera) in this guide (see pp. 104–105)

Stream Cruiser, Male

Common Names of Genera in This Guide: River cruisers (*Macromia* spp.), stream cruisers (*Didymops* spp.)

Emerald Family
Corduliidae

Size: Medium to large

Wings: Most with clear wings; some with amber wash or brown patches in wings

Coloration: Mostly brown or black with yellow spots or stripes; often with green or bronze iridescence

Eyes: Meet broadly along a seam; often brilliant green

Perch: Most hang vertically or obliquely; a few species perch horizontally on the ground or on tree trunks

Flight: Fliers (one genus includes perchers that fly at low to medium heights); fly at medium to high heights

Habitat: Sphagnum bogs, streams, lakes; may feed in swarms over fields and clearings

Miscellaneous: Males often have spindle-shaped abdomens; many species are rare and difficult to observe; many have

American Emerald, Male

northern distributions; females either lack ovipositors or have spoutlike ovipositors and lay eggs in water while alone

49 species (7 genera) in North America
5 species (3 genera) in this guide (see pp. 106–111)

Common Names of Genera in This Guide: American Emerald, baskettails, striped emeralds

38

Skimmer Family
Libellulidae

Size: Small to large

Wings: Clear or conspicuous wing patterns

Coloration: Colorful; males and females often differ noticeably from each other

Eyes: Meet broadly along a seam

Perch: Horizontally, vertically, or obliquely; on vegetation, tree trunks, rocks, or the ground

Flight: Perchers (a few species are fliers); fly at low to high heights

Twelve-spotted Skimmer, Male

Habitat: A wide variety of habitats, especially ponds and marshes

Miscellaneous: Most common, diverse, and easily observed group of dragonflies; females either lack ovipositors or have spoutlike ovipositors, and they lay eggs in water while alone, in tandem, or with the male guarding nearby; some species are migratory

105 species (26 genera) in North America
42 species (12 genera) in this guide (see pp. 112–155)

Common Names of Genera in This Guide: Amberwings, Blue Dasher, corporals, dragonlets, Elfin Skimmer, king skimmers (*Libellula* spp.), meadowhawks, pennants, pondhawks, rainpool gliders (*Pantala* spp.), saddlebags, tropical king skimmers (*Orthemis* spp.), whitefaces, whitetails

Identification Pages

Ebony Jewelwing
Calopteryx maculata 2.0"

I.D.: A large, stunning, green damselfly with satiny black wings. MALE: **Body brilliant iridescent green** (appearing blue in some light). **Wings entirely black.** Legs very long and black. FEMALE: Body more bronzy than male's. Wings brownish with prominent white stigmas.

Behavior: Percher. Perches on streamside vegetation, making periodic forays over the water. Wingbeats slow; **flight bouncing and butterfly-like.** Males perform fluttering courtship displays in front of females. Male guards female as she deposits eggs in floating or submerged vegetation.

Habitat: A variety of streams and rivers; most common on shallow shaded streams with emergent vegetation.

Flight Season: Spring–summer.

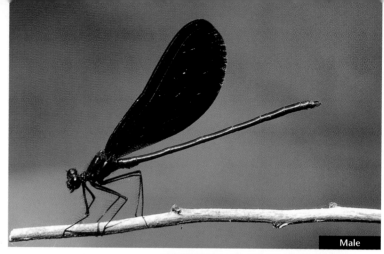

Male

Female

42

River Jewelwing
Calopteryx aequabilis 2.0"

Male

I.D.: A large strikingly green damselfly of northern streams. MALE: **Body brilliant, iridescent green** (appearing blue in some light). Wings clear, **tipped with black** (outer third). Legs very long and black. FEMALE: Body more bronzy than male's. Wingtips brown with prominent white stigmas.

Sparkling Jewelwing (*C. dimidiata*) of the southeastern states has less black in wingtips.

Behavior: Percher. Perches on streamside vegetation or rocks. Wingbeats very slow and butterfly-like. Males perform courtship flight in front of females.

Habitat: A variety of streams and rivers, especially swift and somewhat rocky streams.

Flight Season: Late spring–early summer.

Female

43

American Rubyspot
Hetaerina americana 1.7"

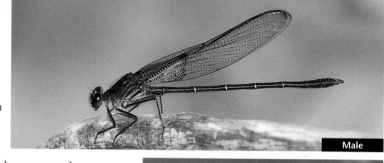

Male

I.D.: A large iridescent damselfly inhabiting streams. MALE: Thorax reddish above and on sides, with thin pale stripes. Abdomen bronzy green. Wings clear or dusky, with large **red patch at base.** Very long blackish legs. FEMALE: Thorax and abdomen green above; abdomen stouter than male's. Wing patch variable: duller red than male's or occasionally dull golden or brown.

Behavior: Percher. Perches on streamside vegetation or exposed rocks. Rarely wanders far from shoreline. Wingbeats are slow and butterfly-like. Males circle each other in display flights. Unlike most damselflies, females are frequently seen at the breeding sites. Females lay eggs

underwater on submerged vegetation or rotting wood while male guards site.

Habitat: Sunny sections of streams and rivers with emergent vegetation and generally moderate flow.

Flight Season: Summer–early fall.

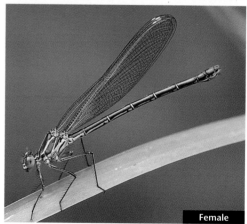

Female

Smoky Rubyspot
Hetaerina titia 1.9"

Male

I.D.: A large, dark, riverine damselfly. MALE: Thorax blackish, with dull red iridescence. **Abdomen black. Wings variable, from smoky black to nearly clear,** with a large reddish patch at base. Legs very long and black. FEMALE: Thorax dark, with green markings. Abdomen variable from greenish to dark brown. Wings with tiny white stigmas (sometimes lacking).
• Male's reddish wing patch and black body are distinctive.

Behavior: Percher. Perches on streamside vegetation and rocks, with periodic swift, erratic flights over the water. Rather wary. Males perform aggressive flight display in which two individuals face each other in up-and-down flight. Females lay eggs underwater on submerged wood and vegetation.

Habitat: Streams and rivers.

Flight Season: Spring–fall.

Common Spreadwing
Lestes disjunctus 1.6"

I.D.: A rather large damselfly of ponds and marshes. **Wings held partially open.** MALE: Thorax dark gray to black above, with thin greenish shoulder stripes, pale below; becomes all pruinose (waxy) gray in older males. Abdomen bronzy above, with grayish blue tip, and grayish base in older males. Eyes and face blue when mature. FEMALE: Thorax blackish above, with thin pale shoulder stripes and light grayish, tan, or yellowish sides. Abdomen bronzy brown above.

Two forms, one northern, one southern, may represent separate species but are not separable in the field. Both the Sweetflag Spreadwing (*L. forcipatus*) and the Lyre-tipped Spreadwing (*L. unguiculatus*) are nearly identical; neither is safely separable, except in the hand.

Male

Behavior: Percher. Male spreadwings spend long periods quietly perched obliquely on emergent vegetation, flying only briefly. Female spreadwings appear at wetlands only when ready to breed. Egg laying done in tandem in stalks of emergent vegetation, a few inches above the water's surface, the female slicing into the plant with the ovipositor near the tip of her abdomen.

Habitat: A variety of still-water habitats, some temporary, including small vegetated ponds, marshes, bogs, vernal pools, and even sluggish streams.

Flight Season:
Spring (southern form)–early fall.

Common Spreadwing, Female

Identifying Common Spreadwings (genus *Lestes*)

Although recognition of spreadwings as a group is fairly easy, based upon their relatively large size and open-winged, oblique perching posture, separation of the 16 *Lestes* species in North America (known collectively as common spreadwings) is difficult and often not possible in the field. Males can sometimes be distinguished by a combination of size and dorsal coloration, but in many cases examination of the distinctive abdominal appendages is necessary. Females are particularly challenging, often difficult to identify even in the hand, and most are best identified simply as "spreadwing species."

Spotted Spreadwing
Lestes congener 1.5"

Male

I.D.: A late-season, medium-sized damselfly of ponds and pools. **Wings held partially open.** MALE: Thorax **black** above, with thin pale shoulder stripes; sides pale blue-gray, with **black spots on lower sides** (difficult to see in the field). Abdomen black above, paler below, with light bluish-gray tip. Eyes blue. FEMALE: Very similar to Common Spreadwing (p. 46) and other small spreadwings, but black spots on lower thorax distinctive.

Behavior: Percher. Perches obliquely on emergent vegetation, generally flying only short distances. Egg laying done in tandem above the waterline on vertical stalks of emergent vegetation, the female depositing eggs by slicing into the plant with her ovipositor.

Habitat: A variety of wetlands, including large marsh-bordered lakes, small vegetated ponds, vernal pools, swamps, and occasionally sluggish backwaters of streams.

Flight Season: Late summer–fall.

Emerald Spreadwing
Lestes dryas 1.4"

Male

I.D.: A medium-sized, stocky green damselfly. **Wings held partially open.** MALE: Thorax bright **metallic green** above, with paler shoulder stripes; pale yellowish to pale blue sides. Abdomen bright **bronzy green above,** with bluish-gray tip. Eyes and face blue. FEMALE: Duller than male and similar to other small spreadwings, though often very greenish above.

Swamp Spreadwing (*L. vigilax,* p. 50) and Elegant Spreadwing (*L. inaequalis*) are larger and usually duller green.

Behavior: Percher. Perches obliquely on the vertical stalks of emergent vegetation. Flight rather weak and typically brief. Egg laying done in tandem above the waterline in stalks of emergent vegetation.

Habitat: A variety of vegetated still-water habitats, often acidic and/or temporary, including small ponds, marshes, and the sluggish backwaters of streams.

Flight Season: Early summer.

Swamp Spreadwing
Lestes vigilax 1.9"

Male

I.D.: A large bronzy-green damselfly. **Wings held partially open.** MALE: Thorax dark above, with greenish iridescence and thin pale shoulder stripes; pale yellowish below. Abdomen **bronzy green above,** with pale blue spot near tip. Eyes and face bluish. FEMALE: Dull brown, often with greenish tinge.

The Elegant Spreadwing (*L. inaequalis*) is somewhat larger and brighter, but difficult to distinguish in the field.

Behavior: Percher. Perches obliquely, low on emergent or shoreline vegetation, flying only short distances. Females appear at water only when ready to breed. Egg laying done in tandem above the waterline in stalks of emergent vegetation.

Habitat: Primarily small well-vegetated ponds, but also marshes, swamps, and sluggish backwaters.

Flight Season: Summer.

Male

I.D.: A large damselfly with a **very long thin abdomen. Wings held partially open.** MALE: Thorax blackish above, with pale shoulder stripes; pale yellowish below. Abdomen entirely dark bronzy, with **no pale spot at tip.** Eyes and face blue. Male appendages curve downward in side view. FEMALE: Duller, with stockier abdomen. • The long slender abdomen of the male, almost twice the length of the wings, is distinctive among the spreadwings.

Behavior: Percher. Often encountered well away from water, perched low in vegetation along woodland roads and trails. Typically avoids open water, preferring shady areas. Female lays eggs alone or in tandem with male, in vertical stalks of emergent vegetation.

Habitat: Breeds in a variety of slow-water habitats, some temporary and often shaded, including small vegetated ponds, marshes, and vernal pools.

Flight Season: Summer.

Great Spreadwing
Archilestes grandis 2.2"

Male

I.D.: The **largest North American damselfly. Wings held partially open when perched.** MALE: Thorax dull greenish bronze above, with distinctive **broad, diagonal, yellowish stripe on sides.** Abdomen dark, with bluish-gray tip. Eyes and face blue. FEMALE: Similar, but browner on body.

The California Spreadwing (*A. californicus*) of the Southwest is very similar but smaller, and the thorax stripe is white and less distinct.

Behavior: Percher. Perches on streamside vegetation, making infrequent brief flights over the water. Females lay eggs in the woody stems of emergent or overhanging vegetation.

Habitat: Sluggish streams, often with alder or willow; also ponds and temporary pools. Once known only from the Southwest, has spread across much of U.S.

Flight Season: Summer–fall.

Aurora Damsel
Chromagrion conditum 1.4"

I.D.: A black-and-blue damselfly, resembling a bluet, but **often holds wings partially open** like a spreadwing. MALE: Thorax black above, blue on sides, with distinctive **yellow patch on lower sides.** Abdomen black, with thin pale rings and blue tip; blue tip has tiny paired black spots separated by thin black lines. FEMALE: Somewhat duller, but with distinctive yellow patch on lower sides.
• Similar to some dark bluets, but yellow patch on lower sides is unique.

Behavior: Percher. Perches, usually obliquely, on vegetation with wings partially spread. Rather sedentary. Egg laying done in tandem on submerged or floating vegetation, the female horizontal and the male nearly vertical.

Male

Habitat: Small vegetated streams, swamps, spring pools.

Flight Season: Spring–early summer.

Male

Familiar Bluet
Enallagma civile 1.4"

I.D.: A medium-sized blue-and-black damselfly. MALE: Thorax mostly blue, with black dorsal and shoulder stripes. Abdomen blue, with black markings; **black most extensive on sixth and seventh segments** (though variable in extent); segments 8 and 9 entirely blue. Eyes with **eyespots, usually small and round or comma-shaped,** but variable in both size and shape. Pale areas on young males are tan or pale lavender, becoming blue with maturity. FEMALE: Thorax tan or pale blue to lavender, with black dorsal stripe and black shoulder stripes. Abdomen black above, pale blue or tan below. Eyes with small blue eyespots.

Very similar to several other bluets, especially the Big Bluet (*E. durum*), Tule Bluet (*E. carunculatum*), and Atlantic Bluet (*E. doubledayi*); differences are subtle, and identification usually requires in-hand examination.

Behavior: Percher. Perches horizontally on the ground, logs, or emergent vegetation. Plucks insect prey from the surface of vegetation in flight. Males make lengthy flights out over open water, just above the surface. Females are generally scarce at wetlands, appearing only when ready to breed. Egg laying done in tandem on submerged vegetation, the female becoming completely submerged but the male releasing the female before he too becomes submerged.

Habitat: A large variety of habitats, including poorly vegetated lakes and ponds, sluggish rivers. Tolerant of brackish, even saline conditions.

Flight Season: Summer.

Female

Identifying Bluets (genus *Enallagma*)

At least 35 species of bluets are known from North America, presenting the novice with a bewildering identification challenge. The males of most species are colored in various combinations of blue and black, but some are extensively red, orange, yellow, or lavender. Although the identification of closely related species often requires examination of the males' abdominal appendages, the males of many species can be separated in the field by a combination of size, coloration, relative extent of black on the abdomen, and the size and shape of the eyespots. Females generally are duller and have more black on the abdomen than males, and are much more difficult to identify, though some have distinctive abdominal patterns.

You will have to examine many individuals in the hand to gain familiarity with this complex group.

Northern Bluet
Enallagma cyathigerum 1.4"

Male

I.D.: A medium-sized black-and-blue damselfly. MALE: Thorax blue, with a broad black dorsal stripe and thinner black shoulder stripes. Abdomen mostly blue, with broad black rings on middle segments, extensive black on segments 6 and 7, and entirely blue segment 8. Eyes with **large blue eyespots.** FEMALE: Duller; pale areas pale blue or brown; abdomen mostly black above.

Difficult to separate in the field from several other species of large blue-and-black bluets, especially the Boreal Bluet (*E. boreale*) of northern climes.

Behavior: Percher. Perches horizontally or obliquely on vegetation. Egg laying done in tandem on submerged or floating vegetation.

Habitat: Small well-vegetated ponds, bog ponds, vernal pools, swamps, and occasionally sluggish streams.

Flight Season: Spring–summer.

Marsh Bluet
Enallagma ebrium 1.2"

I.D.: A small blue-and-black damselfly. MALE: Thorax mostly blue, with broad black dorsal stripe and thinner black shoulder stripes. Abdomen blue, with black markings, most extensive on segments 6 and 7; segments 8 and 9 entirely blue. Eyes with **very small eyespots.** FEMALE: Duller, with abdomen mostly black above.

Not safely separable in the field from several other small bluets, especially Hagen's Bluet (*E. hageni*).

Behavior: Percher. Perches horizontally or obliquely on vegetation. Females lay eggs in tandem or alone, on floating or emergent vegetation, often becoming completely submerged.

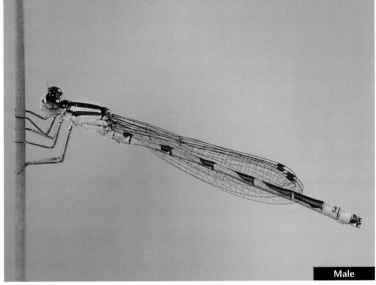

Male

Habitat: Marshes and well-vegetated ponds; generally avoids acidic conditions.

Flight Season: Summer.

Stream Bluet
Enallagma exsulans 1.3"

I.D.: A small black-and-blue damselfly of streams and rivers. MALE: Thorax black above, with thin blue shoulder stripes; mostly blue on sides. **Abdomen mostly black, with thin blue rings;** segment 9 (only) all blue. **Eyespots small and connected,** forming a thin bar. FEMALE: Similar, but more greenish on thorax.

The similar Turquoise Bluet (*E. divagans*) of the Southeast lacks thin blue rings on abdomen.

Behavior: Percher. Perches horizontally or obliquely on emergent vegetation, logs, rocks, or shoreline. Males fly along bank, occasionally hovering a foot or two over the water. Egg laying done in tandem, on submerged or floating vegetation.

Male

Habitat: Medium to large streams and rivers with moderate flow; also large windswept lakes.

Flight Season: Summer.

Skimming Bluet
Enallagma geminatum 1.0"

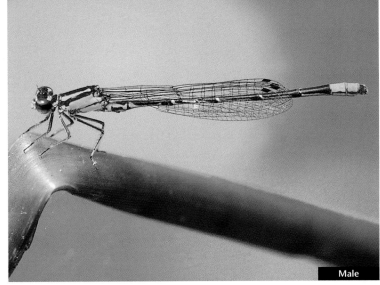

Male

I.D.: A small blue-and-black damselfly of vegetated wetlands. MALE: Thorax blue, with black dorsal and shoulder stripes. **Abdomen mostly black,** with segments 8 and 9 entirely blue above; segment 2 is black above and below, with **blue hourglass-shaped sides.** Eyes with **small, teardrop-shaped, blue eyespots.** Pattern on segment 2 is distinctive, though hard to see in the field. FEMALE: Similar but duller, and abdomen mostly black above.

Behavior: Percher. Perches horizontally on vegetation, especially flat on lily pads. Flies very low, "skimming" the water's surface. Females lay eggs in tandem or alone, on floating or submerged vegetation.

Habitat: Small well-vegetated ponds, often with water lilies, and slow vegetated streams.

Flight Season: Summer.

Azure Bluet
Enallagma aspersum 1.2"

Male

I.D.: A small black-and-blue damselfly. Appears **"black in the middle and blue at both ends."** MALE: Thorax blue, with broad black dorsal stripe and thinner black shoulder stripes. Abdomen mostly black above on middle segments, with all-blue segments 8 and 9. **Segment 7 is blue rearward,** black forward. Eyes with **very large blue eyespots.** Pattern on seventh segment is distinctive. FEMALE: Abdomen mostly black, similar to other female bluets.

Behavior: Percher. Perches horizontally or obliquely on vegetation. Males fly low out over open water. Egg laying done in tandem, on floating or submerged vegetation.

Habitat: Well-vegetated ponds (usually fishless), boggy pools, vernal pools.

Flight Season: Spring–summer.

Taiga Bluet
Coenagrion resolutum 1.2"

I.D.: A small blue-and-black northern damselfly. MALE: Thorax black above, with thin blue shoulder stripes (occasionally broken); **greenish blue on sides.** Abdomen **equally blue and black on first four segments,** mostly black on segments 5–7, and all blue on segments 8 and 9. Blue eyespots. FEMALE: Similar but duller, and abdomen mostly black above.

Greenish tinge on sides of thorax and abdominal pattern distinguish males from most other bluets. The Prairie Bluet (*C. angulatum*) of the northern Midwest and western Canada and Subarctic Bluet (*C. interrogatum*) of Canada are very similar but have less green on thoraxes and subtly different abdominal patterns.

Behavior: Percher. Perches horizontally low on emergent vegetation. Egg laying done in tandem, on emergent or floating vegetation.

Male

Habitat: Marshes, pools, sloughs, and small well-vegetated ponds.

Flight Season: Spring–summer.

61

Orange Bluet
Enallagma signatum 1.3"

I.D.: A medium-sized orange-and-black damselfly. MALE: Thorax **orange,** with black dorsal and shoulder stripes. Abdomen mostly black above, with orange or yellow rings; **segment 9 all orange.** Eyes black above, orange below, with very small **orange eyespots connected, forming a thin bar.** FEMALE: Pale areas dull grayish blue when young, becoming dull yellow with age.

Indistinguishable in the field from the Florida Bluet (*E. pollutum*) of the Southeast. Some immature female forktails are similar but lack all-orange segment 9 and eyespots are not connected.

Behavior: Percher. Perches horizontally or obliquely on emergent and shoreline vegetation, logs, or shoreline. Flies very low over water's surface. Most active late in the day.

Male

Habitat: A variety of still-water habitats as well as sluggish streams. Seems relatively tolerant of disturbed habitats.

Flight Season: Summer.

Vesper Bluet
Enallagma vesperum 1.3"

I.D.: A striking, yellow-and-black, crepuscular damselfly. MALE: Thorax **yellow,** with black dorsal and shoulder stripes. Abdomen mostly black above, pale yellow below, with thin yellow rings; **segment 9 entirely blue.** Eyes dark above, dull orange-yellow below, with fused **yellow eyespots forming a thin bar.** FEMALE: Similar but duller, and with no blue tip on the abdomen.

Very similar to Golden Bluet (*E. sulcatum*) of the Southeast, which has more black on thorax.

Male

Behavior: Percher. Perches horizontally, usually flat on lily pads or other floating plants; occasionally obliquely. Flies very low, skimming the water's surface. Crepuscular, though occasionally active on warm cloudy days. Egg laying done in tandem, possibly after dark, on floating vegetation.

Habitat: Ponds, lakes, and slow vegetated streams.

Flight Season: Summer.

63

Variable Dancer
Argia fumipennis 1.2"

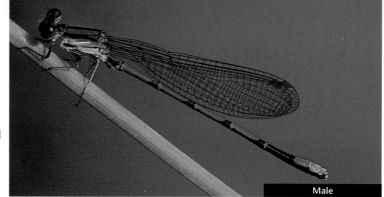

Male

I.D.: A lovely, small, lavender-and-black damselfly. MALE: **Thorax violet,** with thin black dorsal stripes, paler on sides. **Abdomen violet,** with black markings and blue tip; black most extensive on segment 7. Eyes dark, with purple eyespots. Appearance quite variable geographically. Southeastern race has black wings and abdomen mostly black with blue tip.

FEMALE: Thorax light brown or tan, with black stripes. Abdomen brown, with black spots and streaks on the sides. Eyes brownish gray. Through most of the range females are very similar to other dancers and often difficult to separate in the field.

Behavior: Percher. Perches horizontally on rocks, logs, shoreline, and emergent vegetation. Egg laying done in tandem at the water's surface, on floating vegetation, the female typically horizontal, the male nearly vertical, the tip of his abdomen clasping the back of the female's head.

Male, Dark-winged Form

Occasionally many pairs deposit eggs together in small patches of suitable habitat, forming dense breeding congregations.

Habitat: A variety of habitats, but most commonly on vegetated streams and small ponds.

Flight Season:
Spring–summer.

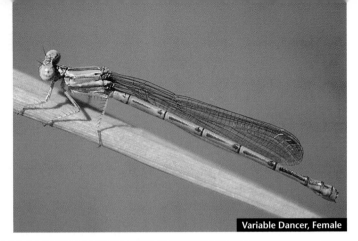

Variable Dancer, Female

Identifying Dancers (genus *Argia*)

The 30 species of dancers in North America (and many more in the tropics) present a difficult identification challenge. They are very similar in appearance to many other pond damsels, especially the bluets (genus *Enallagma*), and are generally most easily distinguished as a group in the field by their distinctive bouncing ("dancing") flight. The males are typically colored in various combinations of blue, lavender, and black, while the females are often drab brown, though in some species a blue form female occurs. Males can often be identified in the field by a combination of size and color pattern. Most females (and some males), however, must frequently be identified simply as "dancer species."

Vivid Dancer
Argia vivida 1.4"

Male

I.D.: A bright blue and black damselfly. MALE: Thorax bright blue above, with broad black dorsal stripe and thin (occasionally broken) black shoulder stripes; blue sides. Abdomen blue, with broad black rings and **black triangles** on sides; last three segments all blue. Eyes dark blue, with pale blue or purple eyespots. FEMALE: Brownish or blue, similar to other dancers.

Abdominal pattern distinguishes this species from the bluets. Emma's Dancer (*A. emma*) of the western states is violet in color. The Springwater Dancer (*A. plana*) of the Midwest and Southwest is very similar and not safely separable in the field.

Behavior: Percher. Perches on rocks, logs, shoreline, and emergent vegetation.

Habitat: Small vegetated pools, streams, and seeps, often spring-fed.

Flight Season: Summer.

Blue-ringed Dancer
Argia sedula 1.3"

I.D.: A handsome, small, dark damselfly with blue-ringed abdomen. MALE: Thorax blue, with black dorsal and shoulder stripes. **Abdomen mostly black, with narrow blue rings** and blue tip (last three segments). Wings often with amber tint. Eyes with blue eyespots. FEMALE: Dull brownish, similar to other female dancers.

Behavior: Percher. Perches horizontally on vegetation or flat surfaces, frequently in the shade. Egg laying done in tandem, on floating vegetation, the female horizontal, the male nearly vertical, supported only by the tip of his abdomen. Occasionally many pairs deposit eggs together in large, often mixed-species groups.

Male

Habitat: Slow (usually) vegetated streams and rivers; occasionally lakes.

Flight Season: Summer.

Blue-fronted Dancer
Argia apicalis 1.4"

Male

I.D.: A striking black-and-blue damselfly. MALE: **Top of thorax bright blue, with very thin black shoulder stripes;** sides of thorax blue or black, depending upon color form. Abdomen black, with last three segments mostly blue. Eyes blackish, with tiny blue eyespots. FEMALE: Occurs in both blue and brown forms, similar to Powdered Dancer (p. 69).

Behavior: Percher. Perches horizontally on rocks, shoreline, or vegetation. Males are territorial, flicking their wings at and chasing intruding males. Flight is bouncy. Egg laying done in tandem, sometimes in groups of pairs, on floating vegetation.

Habitat: Broad muddy rivers and lakes; occasionally smaller ponds.

Flight Season: Summer.

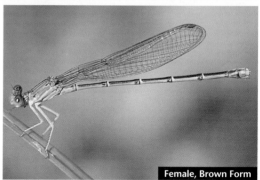

Female, Brown Form

Powdered Dancer
Argia moesta 1.4"

Male

I.D.: A large powder-gray and black damselfly. MALE: Thorax **chalky white,** with dark stripes that become obscured with age. Abdomen blackish, with pale **gray tip.** Eyes dark. FEMALE: Both brown and blue color forms. • The chalky white coloration on the male's thorax is distinctive among damselflies.

Behavior: Percher. Perches on rocks, logs, and sandy shorelines. Egg laying done in tandem on submerged algae-covered rocks or wood, the pairs sometimes completely submerging for up to an hour. Many pairs may deposit eggs together, forming dense breeding congregations.

Habitat: Moderate to large rivers, and large windswept lakes.

Flight Season: Summer.

Female, Blue Form

Eastern Forktail
Ischnura verticalis 1.1"

Western Forktail
Ischnura perparva 1.1"

Eastern Forktail, Male

I.D.: Small green, black, and blue damselflies. MALE: Thorax black above, with **green shoulder stripes; pale green sides.** Abdomen mostly **black, with blue tip** (segments 8 and 9) and thin pale rings; black spots on sides of blue tip. Eyes dark above, greenish below, with small green eyespots. FEMALE: Mature females **powdery grayish-blue** throughout, with black markings absent or obscured; eyespots pale blue. Immature female **thorax bright orange,** with black dorsal and shoulder stripes; abdomen orange at base and **black above, with no blue or orange at tip;** orange eyespots. The rare malelike female is patterned like the male, though duller. • Western and Eastern Forktails are virtually identical and best told by range.

Behavior: Perchers. Perch horizontally low on vegetation, branches, or the ground, or by clinging to sides of vertical stalks of plants. Rarely venture out over open water. Unlike

Eastern Forktail, Mature Female

most damselflies, females are common at wetlands. Females usually lay eggs alone, in emergent or floating vegetation.

Habitat: A variety of wetlands, but most common at small well-vegetated ponds; generally avoid acidic wetlands.

Western Forktail common on slow vegetated streams. Often seen along woodland trails, basking in sunny patches on ground or in low vegetation. Abundant and widespread.

Flight Season: Spring–early fall.

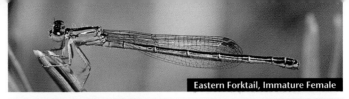

Eastern Forktail, Immature Female

Eastern Forktail, Malelike Female

Identifying Forktails (genus *Ischnura*)

The 14 species of forktails found in North America are distinguished from other pond damsels by a tiny projection extending off the tip of the male's abdomen, though this feature is visible only in the hand. Males generally are various combinations of green, blue, and black and can often be separated by size, the pattern on the top of the thorax (striped vs. spotted), and the relative proportion of blue and black at the tip of the abdomen. Females occur in a bewildering array of orange, green, blue, gray, and black, including a malelike form in most species. Identification of some females is possible by a combination of size and body coloration and pattern.

Rambur's Forktail
Ischnura ramburii 1.2"

I.D.: A green, black, and blue damselfly. MALE: Thorax black above, with **thin green shoulder stripes; pale green on sides.** Abdomen black above, yellowish below; **segment 8 entirely blue.** Eyes black above, greenish below, with tiny blue eyespots. Females occur in three color forms and are very similar to female Eastern Forktails (p. 70). Orange form lacks black shoulder stripes. • Largest of the forktails, with only one (usually) blue segment at tip of abdomen.

Behavior: Percher. Perches horizontally or obliquely on vegetation. Unlike most damselflies, females are commonly seen at wetlands. Females lay eggs alone. Aggressive predator, occasionally taking prey as large as itself.

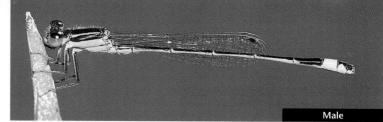

Male

Female, Orange Form

Habitat: A variety of still- or sluggish-water habitats, including brackish ponds and marshes. Primarily coastal in the Northeast.

Flight Season: Spring–fall.

Pacific Forktail
Ischnura cervula 1.1"

Male

Female

I.D.: A small, blue-and-black, western damselfly. MALE: Thorax black above, with **four blue spots,** two forward and two rearward; sides blue. Abdomen is mostly black, except segments 8 and 9, which are mostly blue with black marks on sides. Eyes black above, with tiny blue eyespots. FEMALE: Occurs in two color forms: brown and malelike blue; immatures are pinkish. Shoulder stripes more complete than male's. Abdominal segment 8 mostly blue, with small black spots on sides. Wing stigmas whitish.

The Plains Forktail (*I. damula*) of central North America is very similar and not safely separable in the field; best told by range.

Behavior: Percher. Perches horizontally on vegetation, logs, rocks, or the ground. Rarely flies over open water. Occasionally alights with wings partially open. Females usually lay eggs alone, on floating vegetation.

Habitat: A wide variety of wetlands, including sluggish streams.

Flight Season: Spring–summer.

73

Fragile Forktail
Ischnura posita 1.0"

I.D.: A tiny green-and-black damselfly. MALE: Thorax black above, with **broken green shoulder stripes** (forming exclamation points); mostly green on sides. Abdomen black above, with thin pale rings and **no blue tip** (rarely a blue spot on segment 9). Eyes dark above, greenish below, with tiny green eyespots. FEMALE: Similar to other forktails, but with broken shoulder stripes (though these darken with age and can be difficult to see). • The broken shoulder stripe, and lack of blue abdominal tip in male, are distinctive among forktails.

Male

Behavior: Percher. Perches horizontally on vegetation, often in the shade. An inconspicuous species; lurks low in vegetation, avoiding open water.

Habitat: A variety of wetlands, especially small well-vegetated ponds, vernal pools, swamps, and small vegetated streams.

Flight Season: Spring–summer.

Citrine Forktail
Ischnura hastata 0.9"

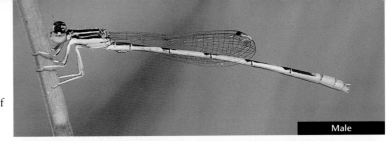

Male

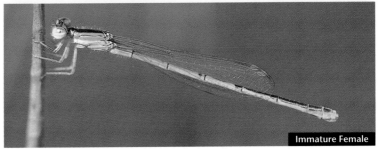

Immature Female

I.D.: A tiny yellow-and-black damselfly of grassy wetlands. MALE: Thorax black above, with **thin yellow or green shoulder stripes;** yellow sides. Abdomen very thin; **mostly yellow, with black markings** above; last three segments all yellow. **Stigmas are differently colored,** reddish on forewing, black on rear wing. Eyes black above and greenish below, with tiny blue eyespots. FEMALE: Orange and black when young, becoming dark bluish gray when mature; similar to several other forktails. • Tiny size, and bright yellow coloration of males, are distinctive.

Behavior: Percher. Perches horizontally on vegetation. Very inconspicuous; skulks low in dense vegetation, never venturing over open water. Despite furtive habits, has been found on many islands far at sea. Females lay eggs alone.

Habitat: Small densely vegetated ponds, vernal pools, and seepage areas, occasionally even brackish wetlands.

Flight Season: Summer.

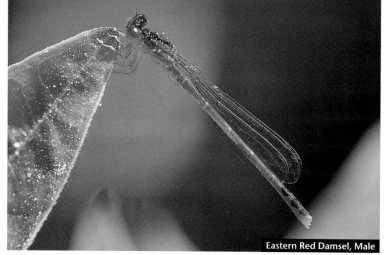

Eastern Red Damsel
Amphiagrion saucium 1.0"

Western Red Damsel
Amphiagrion abbreviatum 1.0"

I.D.: Tiny bright red and black damselflies. EASTERN MALE: Thorax blackish above, **red to orange on sides.** Abdomen **bright red,** with black markings on last four segments. Eyes black above and chestnut below, with no eyespots. EASTERN FEMALE: Similar but duller, with no black on thorax.

Eastern Red Damsel, Male

The WESTERN RED DAMSEL is somewhat larger and stockier, but the two species are not safely separable in the field and are best told by range. Plains population (gray area on map) intermediate. Young females of many forktails are bright orange but are extensively black on the abdomen.

Behavior: Perchers. Skulk about very low in grassy areas, never over open water. Inconspicuous despite bright coloration. Egg laying done in tandem on floating vegetation.

Habitat: Springs and seepage areas at pond, stream, or bog margins.

Flight Season: Spring–early summer.

Eastern   Western

Desert Firetail
Telebasis salva 1.1"

Duckweed Firetail
Telebasis byersi 1.1"

Desert Firetail, Male

I.D.: Tiny bright red or reddish-orange damselflies. MALE: Thorax **mostly red,** with two broad black dorsal stripes. Abdomen **entirely red, with no black markings.** Eyes black on top, chestnut below, with no eyespots. FEMALE: Similar, but rusty brown, with some dark on top of abdomen. • The two species of firetails are virtually identical and identifiable only by range.

Behavior: Perchers. Perch horizontally on floating vegetation. Skulk about low, remaining inconspicuous despite bright coloration. Egg laying done in tandem, on emergent and floating vegetation, especially duckweed.

Habitat: Heavily vegetated ponds, swamps, sluggish streams.

Flight Season:
Spring–summer.

Desert

Duckweed

Sedge Sprite
Nehalennia irene 1.1"

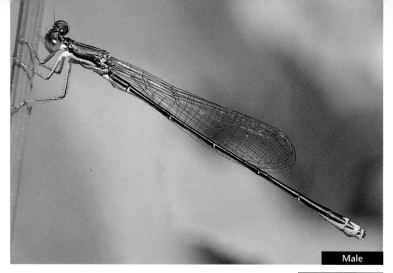

Male

I.D.: A delicate metallic green damselfly of grassy wetlands. MALE: Thorax **iridescent green above,** with no obvious stripes; pale yellow to blue below. Abdomen **green, with mostly blue tip.** Eyes bluish green, with no eyespots. FEMALE: Similar but duller, with less blue on tip of abdomen.

The Sphagnum Sprite (*N. gracilis*) of sphagnum bogs has more blue on tip of abdomen. The Southern Sprite (*N. integricollis*) of the Southeast is slightly smaller, with less blue on segment 8, but difficult to distinguish in the field.

Behavior: Percher. Perches horizontally or obliquely on vegetation. Rarely flies over open water, instead skulking low in dense vegetation, where tiny size and green coloration make them very inconspicuous. Egg laying done in tandem, on floating vegetation.

Habitat: Marshes, marshy ponds, fens, and vernal pools.

Flight Season: Spring–early summer.

I.D.: A **very large** drab gray dragonfly. Thorax **gray, with pale markings** on side. Abdomen **gray, with dark bands and triangles.** Wings clear, with very long narrow stigmas. Eyes grayish, **separated.** Sexes similar. Combination of widely separated eyes, very large size, and drab gray coloration is distinctive.

The Black Petaltail (*Tanypteryx hageni*) of the Pacific Northwest has a mostly black body with yellow spots and markings.

Behavior: Percher. Perches vertically on sunny spots on tree trunks; occasionally on the ground or plant stalks. Flight rather sluggish. Very tame and fearless; will land on light-colored clothing. Feeds on large insects, including butterflies and other dragonflies. Females lay their eggs in mud or decaying vegetation.

Habitat: Seepages, usually on hillsides.

Flight Season: Spring–early summer.

Male

79

Common Green Darner

Anax junius 3.0"

I.D.: A large, active, strong-flying dragon-fly found throughout North America. MALE: **Thorax bright green,** without markings. **Abdomen mostly blue, with black dorsal stripe** that broadens rearward. Eyes olive-green, with a **bull's-eye pattern on forehead.** Wings clear with yellowish to brown stigmas. FEMALE AND IMMATURE MALE: Similar, but **abdomen dull brick-red to violet-red** and eyes brown, occasionally with amber wash in wings.

Combination of unmarked green thorax and blue abdomen is distinctive. Most large darners have striped or mottled sides of thorax. Comet Darner male has brilliant red abdomen (p. 82); female Comet Darner is similar to female Common Green Darner but is larger, has blue eyes, and lacks bull's-eye on forehead.

Male

Behavior: Flier. Males spend lengthy periods flying beats along shoreline 2–3 feet above the water's surface, searching for females and clashing frequently with competing males. Females lay their eggs on floating or submerged vegetation,

usually in tandem with male (unique among darners). Perches by hanging from vegetation, often in grasses low in fields and upland clearings well away from water. Frequently seen flying in feeding swarms 4–20 feet above ground, particularly late in the day and often with other darner species. Some populations highly migratory, with large numbers seen moving along coastlines and inland ridges, especially during the early fall. Feeds on a variety of insects, including other dragonflies, and even has been seen preying on hummingbirds!

Habitat: Breeds in a wide variety of wetlands, including well-vegetated ponds, marshes, and vernal pools. Often seen in upland areas far from water.

Female

Flight Season: Spring–fall. One of the most common and widespread dragonflies in North America, and one of the first and last dragonflies on the wing in northern climes.

Comet Darner
Anax longipes 3.4"

I.D.: A **very large,** striking, green-and-red dragonfly. MALE: **Thorax green,** without obvious markings. **Abdomen brilliant red.** Eyes green. Legs very long, red and black. Lacks bull's-eye pattern on forehead. FEMALE: Duller, with **blue eyes** and more mottled pattern on rusty red abdomen.

Behavior: Flier. Males patrol lengthy beats along shoreline, 3–6 feet above water's surface, frequently interacting aggressively with smaller species and competing males. Unlike most darners, rarely seen when not at breeding sites; does not participate in swarms. Females lay eggs alone, on submerged or partially submerged vegetation.

Habitat: Primarily grassy ponds.

Flight Season: Late spring–summer.

Male

Fawn Darner
Boyeria vinosa 2.6"

I.D.: A large brown dragonfly of shaded streams. MALE: Thorax brown, with **two yellow spots on sides** and indistinct greenish stripes on top. Abdomen brown, with small, indistinct yellow dots on sides. Wings have small brown spots at base and brown stigmas. Eyes dull green. FEMALE: Similar but duller.

The Ocellated Darner (*B. grafiana*) of cold northern lakes and rivers is very similar and not safely distinguished in the field.

Behavior: Flier. Males patrol low over the water, close to shoreline and often in the shade, flying very erratically, exploring any objects they encounter (including dragonfly watchers!). Most active late in the day. Females lay eggs alone, on submerged vegetation or decaying wood, or just above the surface on emergent stalks.

Habitat: Shaded streams, rivers, and poorly vegetated windswept lakes.

Flight Season: Summer–early fall.

Male

Shadow Darner
Aeshna umbrosa 2.9"

I.D.: A large dark brown and blue dragonfly. MALE: Thorax brown, with green to yellow dorsal and side stripes; **side stripes thin, straight, and outlined in black.** Abdomen dark brown, with small blue or green spots, except on segment 10. Eyes dull greenish. FEMALE: Duller, with yellowish markings.

Behavior: Flier. Perches by hanging vertically from vegetation. At breeding sites males patrol over water, close to shore. Females deposit their eggs in wet decaying wood. Often seen flying along edges of fields and clearings or woodland roads, often until dark.

Habitat: Breeds at small, sluggish, shaded streams and at lakes, but often found over upland clearings and woodland roads far from wetlands.

Flight Season: Summer–fall. One of the last dragonflies on the wing in northern climes.

Male

Identifying the Mosaic Darners (genus *Aeshna*)

The mosaic darners comprise 20 very similar species in North America. All are large dark dragonflies with pale blue, green, or yellow markings on the sides and top of the body and clear or amber-tinted wings; the eyes are typically greenish but can be bright blue in a couple of species. Females are very similar to the males but have a somewhat thicker abdomen and two, rather than three, abdominal appendages; these appendages are often broken off in older females.

Identification of the many species is difficult and often requires in-the-hand examination. One of the most useful features is the pattern on the sides of the thorax, in most species consisting of two variably shaped stripes. This feature occasionally can be seen at close range in the field. However, like all darners, the mosaic darners are typically on the wing when encountered, sometimes high overhead, and rarely afford the eager observer much of a view. Even when perched they are often high in a tree. With experience, the subtle distinctions can often be seen in the field, but many sightings must be recorded simply as "mosaic darner species."

Shadow Darner, Female

Cana∂a Darner
Aeshna canadensis 2.8"

I.D.: A large blue-and-brown dragonfly of northern ponds and marshes. MALE: Thorax brown, with blue stripes on top and sides, the **front side stripe with a deep indentation on the front edge.** Abdomen brown, with blue markings on each segment. Eyes blue-green above. FEMALE: Similar but duller, and with three color forms, the pale thoracic markings being either blue (malelike), green, or yellow.

The Green-striped Darner (*A. verticalis*) and Lake Darner (*A. eremita*) are very similar and not safely identified in the field.

Behavior: Flier. Perches by hanging vertically from vegetation. Males patrol shoreline of breeding sites, hovering frequently a few feet above water. Often participates in feeding swarms with other darners over fields and clearings, especially late in the day. Females lay their eggs above the waterline in the stalks of emergent vegetation, slicing into the plant with their ovipositor.

Male

Female

Habitat: Breeds at vegetated ponds, lakes, and sluggish streams, but often found over fields, pastures, and clearings.

Flight Season: Summer–fall.

Variable Darner
Aeshna interrupta 2.9"

I.D.: A large brown-and-blue dragonfly. MALE: Thorax brown, with small (occasionally absent) dorsal stripes; Striped form of central U.S. and Canada has **very thin blue side stripes;** Spotted form of eastern U.S. and Canada and West Coast has **side stripes broken into four spots.** Abdomen brown, with blue spots and markings. Eyes greenish blue. FEMALE: Like male, but three color forms, with pale markings either blue (malelike), green, or yellow.

Behavior: Flier. Perches by hanging from branches and vegetation. Males patrol at breeding sites a few feet over water, close to shore. Often form large feeding swarms over fields and clearings. Females lay eggs above the waterline in the stalks of emergent vegetation.

Habitat: A variety of wetlands, including lakes, boggy ponds, fens, sluggish streams, and even saline ponds. Often found flying over fields and clearings, far from wetlands.

Flight Season: Summer–fall.

Male

Female

87

Blue-eyed Darner
Aeshna multicolor 2.7"

I.D.: A large blue-and-brown dragonfly with bright blue eyes. MALE: Thorax brown, with blue dorsal and lateral stripes; **side stripes relatively straight.** Abdomen brown, with extensive blue markings. **Eyes and face bright blue.** FEMALE: Duller, with greenish eyes, green to yellowish markings, and occasionally a brownish tinge in the wings.

Bright blue eyes distinguish males from most other mosaic darners, except Spatterdock Darner (*A. mutata*) of the Northeast.

Male

Female

Behavior: Flier. Perches by hanging vertically from vegetation. Males patrol a few feet over water's surface, close to shore. Feeding swarms often found flying over fields and clearings. Females lay their eggs above waterline in stalks of emergent vegetation.

Habitat: A variety of vegetated lakes, ponds, and sluggish streams. Often found far from wetlands, and up to several thousand feet in elevation.

Flight Season: Spring–fall.

88

Springtime Darner
Basiaeschna janata 2.4"

I.D.: A large, brown and dull blue, spring-flying dragonfly. MALE: Thorax brown, with short dorsal stripes and **relatively straight dull yellow side stripes.** Abdomen brown, with dull blue markings. Wings with small brown spot at base. Eyes dull blue. FEMALE: Similar to male.

Behavior: Flier. Males patrol along edges of breeding sites, about 2–4 feet above water's surface. Perches by hanging vertically or obliquely from vegetation, often low to ground. Often active until dusk. Does not participate in swarms with other darners. Females lay their eggs in emergent or submerged vegetation.

Habitat: Slow-flowing rivers and streams, lakes and sparsely vegetated ponds.

Male

Flight Season: Spring–early summer.

Cyrano Darner
Nasiaeschna pentacantha 2.7"

Male

I.D.: A large, husky, brown and blue-green dragonfly of shaded southern streams and ponds. MALE: Thorax brown, with green dorsal stripes and **broad, irregular, pale green stripes on sides.** Abdomen dark, with pale green markings on top and sides. **Eyes blue. Forehead projects forward,** noselike. FEMALE: Similar to male, but abdomen thicker.

Behavior: Flier. At breeding sites males patrol with languid back-and-forth flights, 4–6 feet above the water. Perches by clinging vertically to stalks and tree trunks or by hanging from vegetation. Does not feed in the open or in swarms. Prey includes other dragonflies. Females deposit eggs in rotting submerged or partially submerged wood and vegetation.

Habitat: Swamps, wooded ponds, and shaded sluggish streams.

Flight Season: Spring–summer.

Swamp Darner
Epiaeschna heros 3.4"

I.D.: A huge brown-and-green dragonfly of southern swamps. MALE: Thorax brown, with green dorsal stripes and **two green lateral stripes.** Abdomen dark brown, with **green rings** and green patches on the sides. Wings may be tinted with amber. **Eyes bright blue.** FEMALE: Similar to male.

The Regal Darner (*Coryphaeschna ingens*) of the southeastern U.S. is similar, but has more green on thorax and male has green eyes (blue in mature females).

Male

Behavior: Flier. Flies rather leisurely at varying heights over fields and clearings, occasionally in feeding swarms. Perches by hanging from vegetation or clinging vertically to trunks, usually high in trees. Occasionally enters buildings. Males are not territorial at wetlands. Females deposit eggs in emergent vegetation above the waterline, or in shoreline mud. Often preys on other dragonflies. Regularly seen in migratory movements along Atlantic Coast.

Habitat: Swamps, wooded ponds, and shaded sluggish streams.

Flight Season: Spring–early fall (most common in spring and early summer).

Lancet Clubtail
Gomphus exilis 1.7"

Male

I.D.: A medium-sized brown-and-yellow dragonfly. MALE: Thorax brown, with yellow top stripes and **two straight yellow side stripes.** Abdomen brown with **long, narrow, yellow "daggers" running down top;** yellow on sides of narrow club. Eyes bluish gray. FEMALE: Similar, but thicker abdomen without club.

Sixteen closely related species (subgenus *Phanogomphus*) occur in North America, and field identification is not possible in many cases.

Behavior: Percher. Perches horizontally on ground, rocks, and shoreline vegetation. Males make brief patrols very low over water's surface. Over land, males occasionally use undulating flight, roller coasting about 3–6 feet above ground. Females lay their eggs by flying rapidly, low over water, tapping surface repeatedly to release eggs.

Habitat: Vegetated ponds, sandy-bottomed lakes, and sluggish vegetated streams.

Flight Season: Spring–summer.

Lancet Clubtail, Female

Identifying Clubtails (family Gomphidae)

The clubtails are one of the most diverse and challenging groups of dragonflies in the world. At least 98 species occur in North America and more than 1,000 worldwide. They are named for the expansion of abdominal segments 7–9 in many species, which produces a clubbed appearance. This club is more developed in males.

Most clubtails are drably colored in shades of brown, yellow, and green, making them not only inconspicuous but difficult to identify. Additionally, many are wary and/or have habits that make them difficult to find and see well.

If you find a cooperative individual, features to note include its overall size, the width and coloration of the club, color of the abdominal appendages, pattern on the top of the abdomen as well as on the top and sides of the thorax, eye color, and length of the legs. However, for many closely related species, even a good look at all of these features will not suffice; only an in-hand examination of anatomical features will permit certain identification. Even experts must let many pass simply as "clubtail species."

Sulphur-tipped Clubtail
Gomphus militaris 2.0"

I.D.: A medium-sized brown-and-yellow dragonfly of the southern Great Plains. MALE: Thorax dark, with yellow dorsal, shoulder, and side stripes. Abdomen dark, with yellow dorsal stripe; **club mostly yellow,** becoming rusty in some older individuals. Eyes blue. FEMALE: Similar, but without club.

Behavior: Percher. Perches horizontally on the ground, logs, or vegetation. Males patrol low over water away from shoreline. Female lays eggs by flying rapidly, low over water, repeatedly tapping surface with tip of abdomen to release eggs.

Habitat: Muddy-bottomed ponds and lakes, sluggish streams.

Male

Flight Season: Late spring–summer.

Cobra Clubtail
Gomphus vastus 2.1"

I.D.: A medium-sized, blackish and yellow to dull greenish dragonfly with a large club. MALE: Thorax blackish, with broad yellow stripes above; sides mostly yellow (immatures) or pale greenish (adults) with thin dark stripes. Abdomen dark, with short yellow dorsal streaks; **very broad club,** with yellow spots on sides. Base of wings occasionally tinted yellow. Eyes green. Face yellowish, with broad **blackish stripe.** FEMALE: Similar, but with smaller club and pale markings somewhat more extensive.

Immature Male

Several closely related species (subgenus *Gomphurus*) in North America are generally difficult to identify in the field.

Behavior: Percher. Perches horizontally on shoreline or broad leaves of overhanging vegetation. Males make lengthy patrols, 1–2 feet above water's surface, with abdomen tilted upward, periodically hovering and frequently chasing other males. Quite wary.

Habitat: Usually large sandy- or silt-bottomed rivers; occasionally large windswept lakes.

Flight Season: Summer.

Unicorn Clubtail
Arigomphus villosipes 2.0"

Male

I.D.: A medium-sized dull green, yellow, and brown dragonfly. MALE: **Thorax mostly dull grayish green,** with narrow brown dorsal and shoulder stripes. Abdomen mostly dark, with narrow yellow dorsal streaks on first seven segments; **last segment and appendages yellow;** moderate club. Eyes blue-green.

Seven species of *Arigomphus* occur in North America, and separation in the field is often not possible.

Behavior: Percher. Perches horizontally on ground, logs, rocks, lily pads and other vegetation. Males make short low patrols over water with abdomen slightly raised. Females lay their eggs while flying slowly or hovering over water and tapping the surface to release eggs.

Habitat: Mucky-bottomed ponds and lakes; occasionally sluggish streams.

Flight Season: Late spring–early summer.

Common Sanddragon
Progomphus obscurus 2.0"

Male

I.D.: A medium-sized brown-and-yellow dragonfly of sandy ponds and streams. MALE: Thorax brown, with yellow "W" on top and yellow side stripes. Abdomen brown, with broad yellow markings above; club small and dark, with **yellow appendages.** Wings have small dark spot at base and yellowish leading edge. Eyes dull olive. Legs short. FEMALE: Similar but duller, with thicker abdomen.

Four species of *Progomphus* in North America are all similar, and distinction in the field can be difficult.

Behavior: Percher. Perches horizontally on sandy shorelines or, away from water, on vegetation. Males make short fast patrols low over water; more rarely longer patrols with hovering. Females lay their eggs by flying rapidly, low over water, tapping surface with tip of abdomen.

Habitat: Streams and rivers with sandy bottoms; also sandy lakes and ponds in the northern portions of its range.

Flight Season: Summer.

Black-shouldered Spinyleg
Dromogomphus spinosus 2.5"

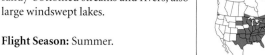

Male

I.D.: A large brown and yellow to dull green dragonfly of streams and lakes. MALE: Thorax mostly yellow (immatures) to dull olive-green (adults), with broad brown shoulder stripes. Abdomen blackish, with a pale yellow dorsal stripe and yellow spots on the lower side; **moderately clubbed** at tip. Eyes green. Legs black; **hind legs very long,** with long spines (difficult to see in the field). FEMALE: Similar, but abdomen not clubbed.

The Southeastern Spinyleg (*D. armatus*) and Flag-tailed Spinyleg (*D. spoliatus*) of the southeastern U.S. are similar, but males of both have rusty-colored clubs.

Behavior: Percher. Perches horizontally on vegetation, rocks, or shoreline. Males make patrolling flights about a foot above the water's surface, periodically hovering with the abdomen cocked upward.

Habitat: Medium to large muddy- or sandy-bottomed streams and rivers; also large windswept lakes.

Flight Season: Summer.

Dragonhunter
Hagenius brevistylus 3.2"

I.D.: A **very large, husky,** black-and-yellow dragonfly inhabiting streams. MALE: Thorax black, with narrow yellow dorsal stripes and two broad yellow side stripes. Abdomen black, with thin yellow streaks above and yellow on the lower sides; **club narrow,** with yellow spots on sides. Head relatively small. **Eyes bright green.** Legs very long. FEMALE: Very similar to male. • Larger than any other clubtails.

Behavior: Percher. Perches horizontally on streamside vegetation or rocks. Males often fly with the tip of the abdomen curled under, forming a distinctive sideways "J" shape. A bold aggressive predator that often preys on other dragonflies, occasionally those nearly its own size, as well as butterflies and other large insects. Females deposit eggs in flight over the water's surface.

Male

Habitat: Shady streams and rivers with moderate to swift flow; occasionally large lakes.

Flight Season: Summer.

Eastern Ringtail
Erpetogomphus designatus 2.0"

I.D.: A medium-sized green, brown, and rusty dragonfly. MALE: Thorax **striped brown and yellow-green.** Abdomen dark brown, with **pale rings;** club is rather small and extensively **rusty orange, with yellow appendages.** Wings have amber wash at base. Eyes grayish blue. FEMALE: Similar, but lacks club.

Six species of ringtails occur in the U.S., and field identification is difficult.

Behavior: Percher. Perches horizontally on shoreline, rocks, or shoreline shrubbery; also perches on the tips of vegetation, skimmerlike. Males patrol by hovering above water's surface, changing positions frequently.

Habitat: Streams and rivers, usually with swift flow and riffles.

Male

Flight Season: Summer.

Rusty Snaketail
Ophiogomphus rupinsulensis 2.0"

Male

I.D.: A medium-sized bright green and brown dragonfly of rivers and streams. MALE: **Thorax brilliant green,** with thin brown shoulder stripes. Abdomen brownish, with dull straw-colored markings; club rather narrow and **usually rust-colored.** Eyes greenish. **Face green.** FEMALE: Similar, but with smaller club and duller abdominal markings.

At least 18 species of snaketails are known from North America, nearly all very similar in appearance. Most lack rusty club, but field identification is tricky at best. Many pondhawks are bright green, but eyes are connected on top of head.

Behavior: Percher. Perches horizontally on rocks, shoreline, or the broad leaves of shoreline vegetation; occasionally "tees-up" on the tips of twigs, skimmerlike. Males patrol low over the water and are often active late in the day.

Habitat: Medium to large swift-flowing rivers and streams.

Flight Season: Spring–early summer.

Twin-spotted Spiketail
Cordulegaster maculata 2.8"

I.D.: A very large, striking, black-and-yellow dragonfly of wooded streams. MALE: Thorax dark brown to black, with yellow dorsal stripes and **two broad yellow side stripes.** Abdomen brown to black, with paired yellow dorsal spots. Eyes bright bluish green and just barely touching on top of head. FEMALE: Similar, but with stockier abdomen and long spikelike ovipositor at end of abdomen. • In southern half of range, both sexes are paler, with blue eyes.

Behavior: Flier. Males patrol low lengthy beats over streams and rivers. Perches by hanging vertically or obliquely from vegetation. Feeds solitarily, low over field edges. Often active early and late in the day. Mating takes place high in trees and can last for several hours. During mating, the female's long ovipositor slides into a deep pocket at the base of the male's abdomen. Females lay their eggs alone, hovering vertically over shallow water or wet mud, rapidly

Male

inserting their spikelike ovipositor into the substrate in a sewing-machine-like movement.

Habitat: A variety of small, clear, shaded streams and small rivers.

Flight Season: Spring–early summer.

Twin-spotted Spiketail, Female

Identifying Spiketails (genus *Cordulegaster*)

The 8 species of spiketails in North America are similar in appearance and generally distinguished by differences in abdominal pattern and range. Depending upon the species, the yellow abdominal markings may form rings, a single row of dorsal spots or daggers, or paired rows of lateral spots or markings.

Most spiketails inhabit very small streams, trickles, and seepages — areas in which few other dragonflies are present. Finding them typically involves waiting patiently for the males to pass upstream or downstream during their lengthy patrols.

Stream Cruiser
Didymops transversa 2.2"

I.D.: A large brown-and-yellow dragonfly. Male: Thorax brown, with a **single yellow side stripe.** Abdomen brown, with pale yellow markings above; clubbed at tip; **appendages dull yellow. Yellow stripe across face.** Wings have dark spot at base and brown leading edge. Eyes greenish when fully mature. Female: Similar, but abdomen less clubbed.

Florida Cruiser (*D. floridensis*) of Florida is very similar, but wings lack basal spots and leading edges are yellow.

Behavior: Flier. Typically found flying fairly low (3–8 feet) along the edges of wooded roads and trails or fields. At breeding sites, males patrol lengthy beats a few feet over water. Perches by hanging vertically or obliquely, often fairly low.

Habitat: Streams, rivers, and lakes, typically with a sandy bottom.

Flight Season: Spring.

Male

Illinois River Cruiser
Macromia illinoiensis 2.8"

I.D.: A handsome, large, black-and-yellow dragonfly. MALE: Thorax dark brown to black, with variable yellow dorsal stripes and bars and a **single yellow side stripe.** Abdomen black, with **bright yellow dorsal spot on segment 7** (yellow dorsal spots on other segments variable within range); slightly clubbed at tip. Eyes bright green when mature. FEMALE: Similar, but with unclubbed abdomen and browner eyes.

About 7 species of river cruisers occur in North America; the taxonomy of some is unclear, and they usually are not safely identified in the field.

Behavior: Flier. Males patrol long beats a couple of feet over water. Forages by flying fairly low and rapidly along dirt roads and trails, or higher and more leisurely over fields and clearings. Perches by hanging vertically, usually high in trees.

Habitat: Rivers and lakes.

Flight Season: Summer.

Male

105

Clamp-tipped Emerald
Somatochlora tenebrosa 2.3"

I.D.: A large, dark, green-eyed dragonfly with elusive, secretive habits. MALE: Thorax blackish, with metallic bronzy and green highlights; sides with a **yellow stripe forward and yellow spot rearward,** which fade with age. Abdomen black and very thin near base. **Appendages clamp-shaped** when viewed from side (often visible in the field). **Eyes bright green** when mature. FEMALE: Similar, but abdomen thicker, lacks distinctive appendages, wings often tinged with amber, and obvious thorn-shaped ovipositor on underside of abdomen.

Behavior: Flier. Forages at varying heights over clearings, fields, woodland roads, and hilltops, primarily early and late in the day. Perches by hanging vertically, usually high in trees. Males patrol shaded streams, with frequent hovering. Females lay eggs in flight by tapping ovipositor against floating vegetation, moss, or soft mud.

Male

Habitat: Very small, often partially dry, shaded streams and brooks. Most frequently seen hawking insects over fields and clearings.

Flight Season: Summer.

Clamp-tipped Emerald, Immature Female

Identifying Striped Emeralds (genus *Somatochlora*)

The 26 species of striped emeralds (genus *Somatochlora*) in North America are primarily northern in distribution, and many have limited ranges. Most are very similar in appearance and can be identified only by the in-hand examination of anatomical features.

When seen, they usually are in flight, appearing as dark slender forms flitting in and out of the shade, difficult to follow, never mind see well. If you are fortunate enough to see one perched, the relative size, pattern of pale spots and stripes on the side of the thorax, and shape of the abdominal appendages may offer some clues to its identity. Otherwise, identification will not be possible beyond "striped emerald species."

Mountain Emerald
Somatochlora semicircularis 2.0"

I.D.: A medium-sized, dark, slender dragon-fly of the Northwest. MALE: Thorax dark brown, with metallic highlights and **two pale yellow oval-shaped spots on sides** which fade with age. Abdomen black. Eyes bright green when mature. FEMALE: Similar, often with some amber in the wing when young.

Behavior: Flier. Males patrol low over vegetated portions of wetlands. Occasionally found flying, at varying heights, over fields and clearings.

Habitat: A variety of habitats, including ponds, marshes, and bogs, often at high elevations.

Flight Season: Summer.

Male

American Emerald
Cordulia shurtleffii 1.9"

I.D.: A medium-sized, dark, green-eyed dragonfly of northern ponds. MALE: Thorax hairy and dark, with dull metallic bronze and green highlights. Abdomen black, with narrow yellow ring near base and dull brown spots on first three segments; **abdomen swollen through segments 6–8,** creating a clubbed appearance. **Eyes bright green** when mature. FEMALE: Similar, but abdomen not clubbed. • Difficult to distinguish in the field from other small emeralds.

Male

Behavior: Flier. Males patrol beat a few feet from shore, hovering frequently, a couple of feet above the surface. Forages along woodland edges. Perches obliquely on vegetation or sometimes flat on a leaf. Females oviposit by flying rapidly over water and tapping surface to release eggs.

Habitat: A variety of vegetated, often boggy, ponds and lakes.

Flight Season: Spring–early summer.

Prince Baskettail
Epitheca princeps 2.8"

I.D.: A large, dark, slender dragonfly with conspicuous wing pattern. MALE: Thorax dull brown and hairy. Abdomen blackish, with dull yellowish rings, which fade with age. Wings with **extensive brown patches at tips, middle, and base** (these markings are considerably reduced in far northern populations). Eyes brown, becoming bright green when mature. FEMALE: Similar. • Darnerlike in size and behavior, but the combination of very large size and wing markings is distinctive.

Male

Behavior: Flier. Forages, frequently in swarms and at treetop level, over roads, fields, and clearings. Often active very early in the morning and late into the evening. Flight consists of rapid wingbeats alternating with brief sails. Perches by hanging vertically, often with the wings partially raised and the abdomen curled upward. Males patrol lengthy beats over water a few feet or more above the surface.

Habitat: Large, often poorly vegetated, ponds and lakes, as well as sluggish streams and rivers with mucky bottoms.

Flight Season: Summer.

Common Baskettail

Epitheca cynosura 1.6"

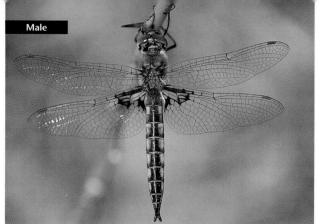

Male

I.D.: A medium-sized, stocky, dull brown dragonfly.
MALE: Thorax brown and hairy, with a dull yellow spot on sides. Abdomen stout and brown, with yellow streaks on sides. **Broad dark triangles** at base of hindwing, but this is lacking in some populations. Eyes brown, becoming bluish with age. FEMALE: Similar.

Most N. Am. baskettails are very similar and often not separable in the field.

Behavior: Flier. Flight rapid and erratic, often in swarms, 4–10 feet above dirt roads and clearings. Perches obliquely low in vegetation. Males patrol shoreline of breeding sites 2–3 feet above surface, hovering frequently. Eggs rolled into a ball (or "basket") under tip of abdomen before releasing, in flight, into water.

Habitat: Ponds, lakes, streams, rivers, marshes. Most often seen over fields, clearings, dirt roads, even parking lots.

Flight Season: Spring.

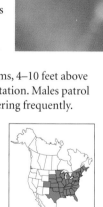

Female, Clear-winged Form

Black Saddlebags
Tramea lacerata 2.1"

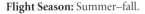
Female

I.D.: A large, dark, broad-winged dragon-fly with conspicuous, large black patch at base of hindwing. MALE: **Black abdomen, with yellow dorsal spots,** most prominent on segments 6 and 7. **Hindwings very broad, with large black patch at base.** FEMALE: Very similar. • Both sexes have long pointed abdominal appendages.

Behavior: Flier. Spends long periods patrolling along pond edges or hawking insects over upland fields and clearings. Flight rather leisurely and bouncy, alternating short bursts of flapping and gliding. Egg laying done in tandem, the male periodically releasing the female, who drops to water's surface to release eggs, then rejoins male. Migratory; often seen in large numbers along the coast or inland ridges, especially from mid-August to mid-October.

Habitat: Breeds at ponds, lakes, and freshwater marshes, but often seen at upland areas well away from water.

Flight Season: Summer–fall.

Red Saddlebags
Tramea onusta 1.8"

Carolina Saddlebags
Tramea carolina 2.0"

Red Saddlebags, Male

I.D.: Large broad-winged dragonflies with conspicuous, large red patch at base of hindwing. MALE: **Red abdomen, with black dorsal spots at tip. Hindwings very broad, with large red patches at base.** FEMALE: Similar but duller.

CAROLINA SADDLEBAGS has more black on tip of abdomen and lacks clear "window" at base of hindwing patch, but otherwise very similar.

Stripes on map show where Red Saddlebags occurs regularly as a vagrant but in small numbers.

Red

Carolina Saddlebags, Male

Behavior: Fliers. Flight alternating bursts of flapping and gliding. Males patrol pond edges, 3–6 feet above surface. Egg laying done in tandem, the male repeatedly releasing the female, who briefly drops down to water's surface, then rejoins male. Forages over upland clearings, often in swarms. Migratory.

Carolina

Habitat: Vegetated ponds and shallow lakes.

Flight Season: Late spring–early fall.

Spot-winged Glider
Pantala hymenaea 1.9"

Male

I.D.: A stocky, broad-winged, brownish dragonfly. MALE: Thorax brown, with dull side stripes. Abdomen brown, with dull rusty and pale mottling. **Hindwings very broad, with small dark patches at base** (often difficult to see); stigmas reddish brown. Eyes reddish brown. Face red. FEMALE AND IMMATURE MALE: Similar but duller, with yellow face.

Behavior: Flier. Spends long periods in gliding flight, interspersing short bursts of flapping, usually about 6–12 feet above ground. Often participates in feeding swarms. Perches by hanging vertically from vegetation, usually a few feet above ground. Many individuals migrate north in spring/early summer to breed; their offspring emerge and fly south in late summer or early fall.

Habitat: Breeds in temporary pools and puddles, rarely brackish. Most often seen over fields, clearings, roads, and even parking lots, well away from water.

Flight Season: Late spring–early fall.

Wandering Glider
Pantala flavescens 1.9"

Female

I.D.: A stocky, broad-winged, golden dragonfly with a strong gliding flight. MALE: Thorax pale brown. **Abdomen tapered and golden orange,** with dark dorsal markings. **Hindwings very broad,** occasionally small amber patch at tip; stigmas orange-brown. Eyes chestnut. Face yellow. FEMALE: Similar, but somewhat duller and more yellowish.

Behavior: Flier. Spends long periods in gliding flight, interspersing short bursts of flapping. Often joins foraging swarms. Perches by hanging vertically on branches and stems, usually close to ground. Wanders long distances in search of rain pools in which to breed; occasionally seen hundreds of miles at sea. Some migrate north in the early summer to breed at northerly latitudes; the young emerge in a month or two, then migrate south in the late summer or fall.

Habitat: Breeds in temporary pools and puddles. Most often seen over fields, clearings, and roads, often well away from water. The only cosmopolitan dragonfly — found on every continent except Antarctica.

Flight Season: Summer–early fall.

Eastern Amberwing
Perithemis tenera 0.9"

I.D.: A very small, stocky, golden dragonfly. One of the smallest dragonflies in North America. MALE: Thorax brown, with thin short dorsal stripes and **yellowish side spots.** Abdomen stout and brown, with pale narrow rings; appendages whitish. Wings **entirely amber, with reddish stigmas;** occasionally brown spots near base. Eyes brown. FEMALE: Body similar to male. Wings usually lack amber coloration and have a **variable pattern of dark patches:** typically a small dark patch on inner wing and a larger band midway out the outer wing. In southern populations, both sexes often have more spotting in wings.

Mexican Amberwing (*P. intensa*) and Slough Amberwing (*P. domitia*) of the extreme Southwest lack distinct spots on thorax.

Male

Behavior: Percher. Perches horizontally on the tips of emergent and shoreline plants. Both sexes are considered wasp mimics. When perched, they often move the wings and abdomen up and down in a wasplike manner. Females fly with abdomen tilted upward and hindwing almost vertical. Males make short patrolling flights low over the water. They choose small territories with floating vegetation and attempt to attract females by hovering over site with abdomen raised. If female accepts, she lays eggs on vegetation just above the waterline, often with the male hovering nearby. The eggs are laid in small clusters that "explode" when they hit the water, dispersing the eggs over the bottom.

Habitat: A wide variety of wetlands, including ponds, lakes, and sluggish streams.

Flight Season: Summer.

Female

Calico Pennant
Celithemis elisa 1.2"

Male

I.D.: A common, small, red-and-black dragonfly. MALE: Thorax blackish, with dull red dorsal stripes. Abdomen **black with red dorsal triangles** and red appendages. Wings with **dark tips, spots at midwing, a dark reddish and brown basal patch on hindwings,** and red stigmas. Eyes dark chestnut. FEMALE AND IMM. MALE: Similar, but yellow where males are red.

Several species of pennants are found in S.E., generally distinguished by wing patterns and coloration.

Behavior: Percher. Perches horizontally on the tips of vegetation. Often seen in fields. At breeding sites, males wait for females, frequently chasing competing males. Egg laying done in tandem, the pair flying over the water and dipping regularly to the surface, where the female taps eggs into the water.

Habitat: Well-vegetated ponds.

Flight Season: Summer.

Female

Banded Pennant
Celithemis fasciata 1.3"

I.D.: A medium-sized black and dark blue dragonfly with spotted wings. MALE: Thorax mostly black. Abdomen **dark navy blue.** Wings with **dark tips, dark bands in the middle, and black basal patches;** wing markings more extensive in southern form. Eyes black. FEMALE AND IMM. MALE: Yellow dorsal spots on abdomen (darken with age), yellow coloration in the basal wing patches, and occasionally pale wingtips.

Male

Behavior: Percher. Usually perches horizontally at the tops of tall shrubs along the shore. Most often seen at water early in the day. Egg laying done in tandem, the pair flying low over the water and repeatedly dipping to the surface.

Habitat: Ponds and lakes.

Flight Season: Summer.

Immature Male, Southern Form

Halloween Pennant
Celithemis eponina 1.5"

Male

I.D.: A medium-sized orange-and-brown dragonfly, butterfly-like in appearance and flight. MALE: Thorax brown, with pale lateral markings. Abdomen dark, with reddish-orange dorsal stripe and reddish appendages. Wings with **dark brown bands, basal spots and bars,** and reddish stigmas. Eyes chestnut. FEMALE AND IMM. MALE: Similar to male, but pale areas yellowish.

Behavior: Percher. "Tees up" on the tips of grasses and low shrubs, often in fields. Wings often held upward, the forewings higher. Flight is bouncy and butterfly-like. Egg laying done in tandem, the pair flying low over the water and dipping to the surface.

Habitat: Breeds at ponds, lakes, and marshes; most often seen in fields, often far from water.

Flight Season: Summer.

Female

Painted Skimmer
Libellula semifasciata 1.7"

I.D.: A striking orange-and-black dragonfly with conspicuous wing pattern. MALE: Thorax brown, with two yellowish side stripes. Abdomen **orange,** with black dorsal triangles on last four segments. Wings with **amber leading edges and tips, dark bars at base, dark patches at midpoint, and dark band near tip.** FEMALE AND IMMATURE MALE: Similar but duller.

Behavior: Percher. Perches horizontally or obliquely on plant stems. Males are territorial at breeding sites, frequently chasing competing males. Often seen in upland areas. Small migratory movements occur periodically along the Atlantic Coast.

Habitat: Well-vegetated ponds and pools; occasionally sluggish streams.

Male

Flight Season: Spring–summer.

Flame Skimmer
Libellula saturata 2.1"

I.D.: A strikingly orange-red dragonfly. MALE: Thorax rusty brown. Abdomen **bright orange-red.** Wings **orange on basal half and leading edge;** stigmas orange. Eyes reddish. Face red. FEMALE AND IMM. MALE: Thorax orangey brown, with yellow dorsal stripe; abdomen orange-brown; wings with amber leading edges.

Neon Skimmer (*L. croceipennis*) of the Southwest is brighter red, with less color in wings (basal quarter only).

Behavior: Percher. Perches horizontally or obliquely on plant stems. Males are territorial; competing males perform lengthy, often very high, side-by-side flight displays.

Habitat: A variety of ponds, lakes, pools, springs, and streams.

Flight Season: Summer.

Male

Female

Golden-winged Skimmer
Libellula auripennis 2.0"

Male

I.D.: A large, bright reddish-orange dragonfly. MALE: Thorax brown. Abdomen **bright orange,** with black dorsal stripe and orange appendages. Wings **tinted orange on front edge,** with reddish stigmas. Eyes rusty brown. Face bright orange. FEMALE AND IMM. MALE: Thorax brown above, with yellow dorsal stripe, dull yellowish sides; abdomen yellow, with black dorsal stripe.

Needham's Skimmer (*L. needhami*) of the Southeast is very similar, but male is more reddish and leading edge of inner wing is dark in both sexes (except in some mature males); it is found in brackish or marshy habitats.

Behavior: Percher. Perches horizontally or obliquely on vegetation. Males are territorial and very aggressive toward competing males.

Habitat: Grassy ponds.

Flight Season: Summer.

Female

Twelve-spotted Skimmer
Libellula pulchella 2.0"

Eight-spotted Skimmer
Libellula forensis 2.0"

Twelve-spotted Skimmer, Male

I.D.: Conspicuous, large, black, gray, and white dragonflies. TWELVE-SPOTTED MALE: Thorax brown, with two yellowish side stripes (becoming obscure with age). Abdomen chalky white. **Wings each have three black patches,** at base, midpoint, and tip; **white patches develop between dark patches** when mature. Eyes brown. TWELVE-SPOTTED FEMALE AND IMMATURE MALE: Thorax brown, with yellowish side stripes. Abdomen brown, with yellow stripes. Wings similar to male's but lack white patches.

EIGHT-SPOTTED SKIMMER of western U.S. is very similar, but lacks dark wingtips in both sexes.

Behavior: Perchers. Perch horizontally or obliquely on shoreline or emergent vegetation. Often encountered at upland fields and clearings. Males are territorial; they make patrolling flights over the water and perform vertical loops with competing males. Females lay their eggs in flight by tapping water's surface with tip of abdomen, occasionally guarded by male. Occasionally small numbers of Twelve-spotted Skimmers are seen in migratory movements of other dragonflies along Atlantic Coast.

Habitat: A variety of ponds, lakes, and sluggish backwaters; occasionally bogs. Eight-spotted Skimmer also in alkaline wetlands.

Flight Season: Summer.

Eight-spotted Skimmer, Male

Twelve-spotted Skimmer, Female

Twelve-spotted

Eight-spotted

Common Whitetail
Libellula lydia 1.7"

Desert Whitetail
Libellula subornata 1.7"

I.D.: Stocky black-and-white dragonflies with broadly banded wings. COMMON MALE: Thorax brown. **Abdomen thick and chalky white.** Wings with **broad black bands across middle,** thick black bars at base. Eyes brown. COMMON FEMALE: Thorax brown, with two pale yellowish side stripes; abdomen brown, with angled yellowish to white dashes on sides. Wings with black patches at base, midpoint, and tips (similar to Twelve-spotted Skimmer, p. 124).

DESERT WHITETAIL male has whitish bases of wings, and black bands have paler central patches. Female has two dark bands across wing, lacks dark wingtips, and has yellow abdomen, with broad black dorsal and lateral stripes.

Common Whitetail, Male

Behavior: Perchers. Perch horizontally on ground, logs, or rocks; also obliquely low on plant stems. Males are territorial and very active at breeding sites; they raise their abdomen in flight in aggressive display toward other males. Females lay eggs in flight, often guarded by male, by tapping tip of abdomen on water's surface.

Habitat: A wide variety of muddy-bottomed ponds, lakes, marshes, and streams. Fairly tolerant of disturbed habitats.

Flight Season: Summer.

Common Whitetail, Female

Desert Whitetail, Male

I.D.: A distinctive black-and-gray dragonfly with boldly marked wings. MALE: Thorax grayish white above, black on the sides. Abdomen becomes **entirely whitish. Broad black bands across base of wings** and **white bands across middle of wings.** Eyes black. FEMALE AND IMM. MALE: Thorax brown, with yellow dorsal stripe. Abdomen yellow, with black dorsal and lateral stripes; wings similar to adult male's, but without white bands; often with a dusky tip.

Behavior: Percher. Perches obliquely on plant stems. Males are territorial at water. At high densities, dominant males are most successful at mating. Often seen in upland fields and meadows, well away from water.

Habitat: Ponds and lakes; occasionally sluggish streams.

Flight Season: Summer.

Male

Female

Four-spotted Skimmer

Libellula quadrimaculata 1.7"

Male

I.D.: A stocky brownish dragonfly of northern bogs and ponds. MALE: Thorax brown and hairy. Abdomen **brown at base, increasingly black toward tip;** narrow yellowish lateral stripe. Wings have **amber bar at base, small black spot at midpoint,** and **black basal patch on hindwing.** Eyes dark. FEMALE: Very similar to male.

Behavior: Percher. Perches horizontally or obliquely on plant stems. Females lay their eggs in flight by tapping water's surface with tip of abdomen.

Habitat: A variety of boggy or marshy wetlands, usually acidic.

Flight Season: Late spring–summer. Distributed throughout boreal (northern) regions worldwide.

Chalk-fronted Corporal
Libellula julia 1.6"

Male

I.D.: A stocky gray-and-black dragonfly of northern ponds. MALE: Thorax **gray above,** brown on the sides. Abdomen **gray at base** (first four segments), remainder black. Wings have **small dark patches at base.** FEMALE AND IMM. MALE: Rusty brown, with pale shoulder ("corporal") stripes and a black dorsal stripe on abdomen.

The White Corporal (*L. exusta*) of the Northeast is similar, but males have all-white abdomen and dark thorax.

Behavior: Percher. Perches horizontally on logs, rocks, floating vegetation, and the ground; occasionally obliquely on plant stems. Often basks in sunny woodland patches.

Habitat: Boggy pools and ponds, swamps, and marshes.

Flight Season: Spring–early summer.

Female

Blue Corporal
Libellula deplanata 1.4"

I.D.: A stocky blue dragonfly. MALE: Thorax and abdomen **mostly dark blue.** Wings with **dark streaks at base** (longer and broader on hindwings). FEMALE AND IMM. MALE: Rusty brown thorax, with two pale shoulder ("corporal") stripes; abdomen rusty, with black dorsal triangles.

Behavior: Percher. Perches horizontally on ground, logs, and rocks; often vertically flat against tree trunks. Males are territorial, frequently chasing other males and making brief patrol flights low over the water.

Habitat: Vegetated, usually sandy-bottomed, ponds and shallow lakes.

Flight Season: Spring–early summer.

Male

Female

Spangled Skimmer
Libellula cyanea 1.8"

Comanche Skimmer
Libellula comanche 2.1"

Spangled Skimmer, Male

I.D.: Large blue dragonflies with conspicuous white stigmas. SPANGLED MALE: Thorax and abdomen entirely blue in mature males. Wings with dark basal streaks, slight amber wash on front edge, and **partially white stigmas.** Eyes dark green. **Face black.** SPANGLED FEMALE AND IMMATURE MALE: Thorax dark brown, with broad yellowish patches on sides; abdomen yellow, with broad black dorsal stripe; wings with white stigmas and dark tips.

COMANCHE SKIMMER males are a bit larger, somewhat grayer, have a white face, and lack dark basal wing streaks. Female very similar to Spangled Skimmer, but wings are less dark at tips and white in stigmas is reduced or lacking.

Behavior: Perchers. "Tee up" or perch obliquely on shoreline or emergent vegetation. Male Comanche Skimmers patrol

Comanche Skimmer, Male

streams in darnerlike fashion. Females deposit their eggs in flight by tapping water's surface with tip of abdomen.

Habitat: Spangled Skimmers at vegetated ponds and shallow lakes; sluggish backwaters. Comanche Skimmers at streams and springs.

Flight Season: Summer.

Spangled Skimmer, Female

Spangled

Comanche

Slaty Skimmer
Libellula incesta 2.0"

Male

I.D.: A common and conspicuous, large, dark dragonfly. MALE: **Thorax and abdomen entirely dark slate blue,** often appearing black. Wings clear, with black stigmas and narrow dark tips. Eyes blackish. FEMALE AND IMMATURE MALE: Thorax brown above, with yellow dorsal stripe, pale yellow on sides. Abdomen yellow, with broad black dorsal stripe. Older females become rather uniform brownish gray.

Behavior: Percher. "Tees up" or perches obliquely on vegetation; occasionally horizontally on logs or rocks. Males are territorial and very aggressive; competing males perform flight displays involving horizontal loops around each other.

Habitat: A wide variety of ponds and lakes; sluggish streams.

Flight Season: Summer.

Female

Great Blue Skimmer
Libellula vibrans 2.2"

I.D.: A large blue dragonfly of southeastern swamps. MALE: **Thorax and abdomen powdery blue.** Wings have small black bars at base, spots at midpoint, black stigmas, and narrow black edges at tip. **Eyes greenish blue.** FEMALE AND IMMATURE MALE: Thorax brown above, with pale dorsal stripe and pale gray sides; abdomen yellow, with black dorsal stripe; wings more broadly tipped with black than male's. Older females become dark grayish throughout, with green eyes.

Behavior: Percher. Perches horizontally or obliquely on plant stems. Males patrol territories along shoreline and hover-guard egg-laying females. Often not wary. Small numbers occasionally participate in migratory movements.

Habitat: Swampy ponds and pools; sluggish shady streams.

Flight Season: Spring–summer.

Male

Female

Blue Dasher
Pachydiplax longipennis 1.4"

Male

I.D.: A rather small blue-and-brown dragonfly, abundant across much of U.S. MALE: **Thorax brown, with yellow striping** (fades with age). **Abdomen blue, with black tip.** Wings often with amber patch of variable size (primarily in eastern populations). **Eyes green.** FEMALE AND IMMATURE MALE: Thorax brown, with yellow striping. Abdomen dark, with distinctive **paired yellow streaks down top.** Wings often with variably sized amber patches. Eyes reddish brown.

Behavior: Percher. Perches horizontally on shoreline shrubs and vegetation, occasionally quite high. Wings often held downward, below horizontal. Males make short patrols over water, hovering frequently, to search for females and chase other males. Competing males confront each other with abdomens raised, each trying to get underneath the other to drive the competitor up and away. Females lay eggs by hovering low over water and repeatedly tapping surface with tip of abdomen. Males guard females from a nearby perch or by hovering nearby. Small numbers sometimes participate in migratory movements of dragonflies along Atlantic Coast.

136

Habitat: Found in a wide variety of habitats, but most common on well-vegetated ponds. Also in open swamps, marshes, sluggish backwaters, bogs, and fields. Apparently fairly tolerant of disturbed or rather polluted waters.

Flight Season: Summer.

Female

Eastern Pondhawk
Erythemis simplicicollis 1.7"

Western Pondhawk
Erythemis collocata 1.6"

I.D.: Common blue-and-black or green-and-black dragonflies of vegetated ponds. EASTERN MALE: **Thorax and abdomen mostly powdery blue;** appendages white. Wings clear, with pale brown stigmas. **Eyes and face green.** EASTERN FEMALE AND IMMATURE MALE: **Thorax bright green. Abdomen green, with black markings,** the black predominating rearward; appendages white. Eyes and face green.

WESTERN PONDHAWK males have stouter abdomens, with black appendages. Females are all green, with a black dorsal stripe on abdomen.

Behavior: Perchers. Perch horizontally on shore, logs, or rocks; less commonly obliquely low on vertical stalks.

Eastern Pondhawk, Male

Voracious predators, occasionally capturing other dragonflies their size, even others of their own species. Competing males perform distinctive flight displays in which each alternately makes vertical loops under then in front of the other, in a leapfrog pattern (these displays are rare in Western Pondhawk). With the male guarding nearby, females lay their eggs by hovering just over the water and repeatedly swinging the abdomen downward to the surface to release eggs.

Habitat: Ponds, lakes, and sluggish backwaters; Western Pondhawk often at hot springs.

Flight Season: Summer.

Eastern Pondhawk, Female

Western Pondhawk, Male

Eastern

Western

Little Blue Dragonlet
Erythrodiplax minuscula 1.0"

Male, in "Obelisking" Posture

I.D.: A small blue-and-black dragonfly of the Southeast. MALE: Thorax mostly black, becoming powdery blue when mature. **Abdomen mostly blue, with black tip; appendages whitish.** Hindwings have small black basal patch. Eyes dark and face black. FEMALE AND IMMATURE MALE: Thorax is yellowish or tan, with broad dark shoulder stripes. Abdomen yellowish to tan, with dark lateral markings and black tip; appendages whitish. Hindwing basal spot amber. Eyes chestnut to dull grayish green.

Behavior: Percher. "Tees up" horizontally on twigs or grasses, often with wings drooped and abdomen cocked upward ("obelisking").

Habitat: Well-vegetated ponds and lakes, sluggish backwaters.

Flight Season: Spring–fall.

Female

Seaside Dragonlet
Erythrodiplax berenice 1.3"

I.D.: A small blackish dragonfly of salt marshes.
MALE: **Thorax and abdomen dark navy blue to
black.** Wings clear. Eyes dark chestnut to black.
FEMALE AND IMMATURE MALE: Thorax with lovely
striped orange-and-black pattern on sides
which darkens with age; abdomen mostly
orange to yellow above, black on the lower sides.
Wings often with an amber patch in middle.
Some females become mostly black like males.

Behavior: Percher. Perches horizontally or
obliquely on marsh grasses; occasionally on the ground.
Males territorial around marsh pools or creeks. Egg
laying done in tandem on algae mats.

Habitat: Salt marshes, saline lakes, and
mangrove swamps. The only dragonfly
that breeds in pure seawater.

Flight Season: Summer.

Male

Female

Elfin Skimmer
Nannothemis bella 0.8"

Male

I.D.: A **tiny** blue dragonfly of northern bogs. MALE: Thorax and abdomen black, **becoming powdery blue** when mature; abdomen slightly swollen near tip. Eyes grayish brown. FEMALE: Thorax brown, with yellow mottling; abdomen black, with **yellow rings and bands, resembling a bee.** Wings amber at base. Eyes brown.

Behavior: Percher. Perches horizontally or obliquely very low on grasses and other plants, often with wings drooped downward. Very inconspicuous; remains within a few inches of the ground. Females lay their eggs in tiny pockets of water in soupy sphagnum mats, often with the male hover-guarding.

Habitat: Bogs and fens.

Flight Season: Summer.

Female

Roseate Skimmer
Orthemis ferruginea 2.0"

I.D.: A large purplish-pink or red dragon-fly. MALE: **Thorax lavender. Abdomen bright pinkish.** Eyes dark chestnut. Also a red form (perhaps a separate species) in which thorax and abdomen are bright red. FEMALE: Thorax brown, with pale dorsal stripe and mosaic of whitish streaking on sides; abdomen mostly rusty brown.

Behavior: Percher. Perches horizontally or obliquely on vegetation. Forages in upland fields and clearings. Male often bends abdomen downward in aggressive or sexual aerial encounters.

Habitat: A variety of ponds, lakes, sluggish streams, and ditches, occasionally brackish.

Flight Season: Spring–fall.

Male

Female

White-faced Meadowhawk
Sympetrum obtrusum 1.3"

Ruby Meadowhawk
Sympetrum rubicundulum 1.3"

White-faced Meadowhawk, Male

I.D.: Small, red-and-black, late-season dragon-flies. MALE: Thorax reddish brown. **Abdomen red, with black triangles on lower sides.** Eyes rusty brown. Face color variable; typically pure white in White-faced, dull straw-colored in Ruby. FEMALE AND IMMATURE MALE: Similar in pattern to male, but pale areas bright yellow (not red) when young, becoming dull olive-brown when mature. • Both species often have small amber patch at base of hindwing; in Midwest, this patch often extensive.

The Cherry-faced Meadowhawk (*S. internum*) of the northern U.S. and Canada is nearly identical but often has a reddish face and (in the West) reddish wing veins.

Behavior: Perchers. Perch horizontally on ground, logs, or rocks, or "teed up" on stalks of vegetation. Will land on light-colored clothing on cool days. Males maintain small territories in grassy marshes. Females usually lay their eggs in flight, either alone with the male guarding nearby or in tandem with the male.

Habitat: A variety of wetlands, including ponds (often temporary), marshes, bogs, and sluggish streams. Often in fields and clearings far from water.

Flight Season: Late summer–fall.

Ruby Meadowhawk, Male

White-faced Meadowhawk, Female

White-faced

Ruby

Identifying Meadowhawks (genus *Sympetrum*)

The red meadowhawks of North America present an intractable field problem. Although some species are recognizable in the field, the identification of many, even in the hand, is difficult at best. The taxonomy of this complex is unclear, and the exact number of species uncertain. The White-faced/Cherry-faced/Ruby complex is particularly troublesome. Although face color can be useful, it can be difficult to see in the field and is not always a reliable indicator. A male meadowhawk with a distinctly white face is probably a White-faced Meadowhawk. Male Cherry-faced Meadowhawks in the West have reddish faces (but beware male Yellow-legged Meadowhawks, p. 146, and Saffron-winged Meadowhawks, p. 148, which can have reddish faces); however, eastern individuals have dull olive-yellow faces, as do Ruby Meadowhawks. A meadowhawk with a dull yellowish or ivory face cannot be identified with certainty in the field.

Yellow-legged Meadowhawk
Sympetrum vicinum 1.3"

I.D.: A small, red-and-brown, late-season dragonfly. MALE: Thorax rusty brown. **Abdomen red, with black markings small or absent.** Eyes dark chestnut. Wings often with small amber basal patches. **Face reddish. Legs brown.** FEMALE AND IMMATURE MALE: Abdomen yellow, becoming dull brown or reddish in older females. Legs yellow in immatures, but become dull brown. Triangular ovipositor of female distinctive among meadowhawks.

• Despite its name, the legs of Yellow-legged Meadowhawk are obviously yellow only in immatures; the legs darken with age, becoming dark brown (but never black as in many other meadowhawks) in older individuals.

Male

Behavior: Percher. Perches horizontally on the ground, logs, rocks, or broad leaves; also vertically on tree trunks or buildings when cool. Egg laying done in tandem in flight, the pair dipping to the water's surface, where the female taps the tip of her abdomen to release eggs. Very confiding; will land on light clothing, especially on cool days. Mass migration-like movements, often involving pairs in tandem, have been observed on occasion during the fall.

Habitat: A variety of ponds, lakes, marshes, and sluggish streams, including temporary pools. Often found in upland clearings and backyards, far from water.

Flight Season: Late summer–fall. Typically the last species on the wing in northern climes.

Female

Saffron-winged Meadowhawk
Sympetrum costiferum 1.4"

I.D.: A medium-sized red dragonfly. MALE: Thorax brown, tinged with reddish. **Abdomen brick red, with little black.** Wings with small amber patch at base of hindwings and **amber wash on leading edges** which fades with age; **stigmas red.** Eyes reddish brown. Legs vary from dull yellowish to black. FEMALE AND IMMATURE MALE: Thorax and abdomen yellow, darkening to brown with age. Amber on leading edge of wing more prominent; stigmas yellow.

Male

Behavior: Percher. Perches horizontally on the ground, logs, rocks, or low vegetation. Males "tee up" on emergent vegetation at breeding sites, making short patrolling flights low over the water. Egg laying done in tandem, the pair hovering a few inches over the water and making frequent dips to the surface.

Habitat: A variety of ponds and lakes, often poorly vegetated, including brackish and acidic wetlands.

Flight Season: Summer–early fall.

Band-winged Meadowhawk
Sympetrum semicinctum 1.3"

Western Meadowhawk
Sympetrum occidentale 1.3"

Band-winged Meadowhawk, Male

I.D.: Small red-and-black dragonflies with amber banded wings. BAND-WINGED MALE: Thorax rusty brown. **Abdomen red,** with irregular black stripe on lower sides. **Hindwings with broad amber basal patch or band,** variable in extent but usually darkest on outer margins. Eyes dark rusty brown. BAND-WINGED FEMALE: Similar, but abdomen yellowish brown, though some become dull red with age.

WESTERN MEADOWHAWK has black "W" pattern on sides of thorax but is otherwise identical. Some Ruby (p. 144) and Cherry-faced Meadowhawks in Midwest have amber basal wing patches and are indistinguishable in the field.

Behavior: Perchers. Perch horizontally on ground, logs, rocks, or "teed up" on vegetation. Egg laying done in tandem. Western Meadowhawk pairs often seen far from water.

Habitat: Marshy wetlands and seepages.

Flight Season: Summer–early fall.

Band-winged

Western

Variegated Meadowhawk
Sympetrum corruptum 1.5"

Male

I.D.: A medium-sized, mottled red, white, and brown dragonfly of the West. MALE: Thorax brown, with pale yellow side stripes, fading to spots in older males. **Abdomen with complex mosaic of red, white, and grayish-brown patches.** Pattern fades with age, older males becoming mostly reddish. **Wings with yellowish leading edges and yellowish-tipped stigmas.** Eyes reddish brown. FEMALE AND IMMATURE MALE: Similar, but abdominal markings yellow when young, becoming red with age. Body pattern often obscure on older females.

Striped area on map shows where species occurs regularly as a vagrant but in small numbers.

Behavior: Percher. Perches horizontally on ground or low vegetation. Males are territorial at water. Egg laying done in tandem in flight. Often found in upland areas far from water. Migratory, with large movements occasionally seen along Pacific Coast. Some wander eastward to Atlantic Coast and Southeast in fall.

Habitat: Breeds at a variety of wetlands, including ponds, pools, slow streams, springs, and saline lakes.

Flight Season: Spring–fall.

I.D.: A small black-and-yellow dragonfly of northern ponds and bogs. MALE: **Thorax black, with yellow side spots** which disappear with age. **Abdomen black, with dull yellow spots.** Eyes and face black. FEMALE AND IMMATURE MALE: More complex and extensively yellow pattern on thorax and abdomen. Wings often with small amber patch at base of hindwing and yellow leading edge.

Behavior: Percher. Perches horizontally on ground, logs, rocks, or vegetation. Often seen at upland clearings some distance from water. Males "tee up" on vegetation at breeding sites, making brief flights low over the water. Egg laying done in tandem, the pair usually flying a few inches over the water and dipping down to drop eggs at the surface.

Male

Habitat: A variety of wetlands, but most common at bogs, marshes, and fens.

Flight Season: Summer–early fall.

Dot-tailed Whiteface
Leucorrhinia intacta 1.3"

I.D.: A common small black dragonfly of vegetated ponds. MALE: Thorax black. **Abdomen black, with distinct yellow dorsal spot near tip** (segment 7). Hindwings have small dark patch at base. Eyes dark. **Face white.** FEMALE AND IMMATURE MALE: Blackish, with yellow markings on thorax and yellow dorsal spots on abdomen. Very similar to other female and immature whitefaces. Older females become very malelike in appearance.

Male

Behavior: Percher. Perches horizontally on ground, logs, or floating vegetation (especially water lilies); also "tees up" on vegetation. Males are territorial. Females lay eggs in flight by tapping water with tip of abdomen, often with the male hovering nearby. Occasionally two males are seen in tandem; it has been suggested that this is one means by which a male prevents a competing male from mating with his mate while she lays eggs.

Habitat: Vegetated ponds and lakes, sluggish backwaters, bogs.

Flight Season: Spring–summer.

Dot-tailed Whiteface, Female

Identifying Whitefaces (genus *Leucorrhinia*)

The whitefaces are closely related to the meadowhawks (genus *Sympetrum*) and are very similar in appearance and behavior. They differ in having bright white faces and small dark basal wing patches, are generally blacker in coloration, and fly earlier in the season. The 7 species in North America can usually be distinguished, given a close look, by the pattern and extent of pale coloration (usually red in males, yellow in females and immatures) on the top of the abdomen and on the thorax. In some cases, similar species cannot be distinguished in the field.

Crimson-ringed Whiteface
Leucorrhinia glacialis 1.4"

Male

I.D.: A rather small black-and-red dragonfly of northern ponds and bogs. MALE: **Mostly black, with red on rear of thorax and base of abdomen.** Hindwings have small dark patch at base. Eyes dark. **Face bright white.** FEMALE AND IMMATURE MALE: Mostly black, with yellow markings on thorax and yellow spots on top of abdomen (becoming red in some females). Eyes dark brown. Face white.

The Red-waisted Whiteface (*L. proxima*) of northern bogs and ponds is very similar and often not distinguishable in the field (especially in the West).

Behavior: Percher. Perches horizontally or obliquely on emergent, floating, or shoreline vegetation; occasionally on ground. Males are territorial. Females deposit eggs in flight by tapping water's surface with tip of abdomen, often while the male hovers nearby.

Habitat: Well-vegetated ponds and lakes, bogs.

Flight Season: Late spring–summer.

Hudsonian Whiteface
Leucorrhinia hudsonica 1.2"

I.D.: A small black-and-red dragonfly of northern ponds and bogs. MALE: Thorax black, with red markings. **Abdomen black, with reddish dorsal spots** on all but last three segments. Hindwings have small dark patch at base. Eyes dark. **Face bright white.** FEMALE AND IMMATURE MALE: Similar, but with yellow, not red, markings. Older females often become quite reddish. Difficult to distinguish from females of some other whitefaces.

Behavior: Percher. Perches horizontally on ground, broad leaves, or floating vegetation; or obliquely on vertical stems. Males guard a very small territory. Females lay their eggs in flight by tapping water's surface with tip of abdomen.

Habitat: Marshy or boggy ponds and lakes, bogs, fens.

Male

Flight Season: Spring–early summer.

Index to Common Names

Index to Scientific Names

Broad-winged
Damsels

Spreadwings

Pond Damsels

Petaltails

Darners

Clubtails

Spiketails

Cruisers

Emeralds

Skimmers